Learning to Learn
Making Learning Work
for All Students

Garry Burnett

www.garryburnett.com

CAMPAIGN
FOR **LEARNING**

Crown House Publishing Limited
www.crownhouse.co.uk

First published by

Crown House Publishing Ltd
Crown Buildings, Bancyfelin, Carmarthen, Wales, SA33 5ND, UK
www.crownhouse.co.uk

and

Crown House Publishing Company LLC
6 Trowbridge Drive, Suite 5, Bethel, CT 06801, USA
www.CHPUS.com

First published 2002.
Reprinted 2002, 2003, 2004, 2007.

British Library Cataloguing-in-Publication Data
A catalogue entry for this book is available
from the British Library.

ISBN 978-1899836789

LCCN 2003102584

Printed and bound in the UK by
Bell & Bain
Glasgow

Isn't it strange?

Isn't it strange, that princes and kings
And clowns who caper in sawdust rings
And ordinary folk like you and me
Are builders of eternity?
To each is given a bag of tools
An hour glass and a book of rules
And each must build ere time is flown
A stumbling block, or a stepping stone.

(Anon.)

Dedicated to the memory of Ellen Gardner who taught us all to think 'we can'.

Table of Contents

Skills for Effective Learning

Acknowledgements

It gives me great pleasure to acknowledge and give thanks to the following people who helped prepare this book:

My wife Louise who showed patience and wisdom with her suggestions for improvements, Jeff Turner for his work on the sound and graphics; Bill Lucas, Toby Greany and Julia Wright at the *Campaign for Learning* for giving Learning to Learn such a high profile; Colin Rose for his inspirational ideas; Kay Jarvis and Sheila Ireland of Malet Lambert School whose continued support gives me strength; all of my friends and colleagues from the associate schools in the *Campaign for Learning* 'Learning to Learn in schools' project, but especially Tony Hinkley of Dudley LEA for his encouragement and belief; and to Bridget Shine and Sam Hemmant at Crown House Publishing for their complete dedication and tolerance.

Foreword

Learning to Learn is the key skill of the twenty first century. In a rapidly changing and uncertain world it has to be the most important element of the curriculum, and I am quite clear that it should be the goal of every school to ensure that all pupils leave knowing how they learn best, ready to face a lifetime of learning with confidence and enjoyment.

Garry Burnett is a teacher who has been trying to do just this over a number of years.

I met him when the Campaign for Learning was scanning the school horizon for innovative practice. Malet Lambert School's work immediately attracted our attention for the way in which it sought to engage both pupils and parents in the learning process.

Over the last two years I have worked closely with him on the national Learning to Learn project of which Malet Lambert School is part. Garry is one of those committed and inspirational teachers who any parent would want to teach their child, and I am delighted to be able to introduce his first book.

Learning to Learn, Making Learning Work for All Students is full of good ideas for teachers and pupils who want to become more effective learners and teachers. The book is rich in stories and songs to inspire, challenge and act as stimulus for discussion. Practical activities also ensure that pupils can experience new techniques at first hand. *Learning to Learn* is a really good starting point for any teacher wanting to develop their own thinking and to try things out in the classroom.

For we all need to remember that learning is learnable....

And the best gift any teacher can give his or her pupils is the confidence and competence to put this belief into practice in their daily lives.

Bill Lucas
Chief Executive
Campaign for Learning

CAMPAIGN
FOR **LEARNING**

Teacher's Section

Teacher's Introduction

For some reason unknown to me, I have great difficulty seeing 'Magic Eye' pictures. The first time I ever came across one, on a balmy evening in Mousehole, near St Ives, I remember spending a conspicuously embarrassing amount of time squinting and pulling faces at what looked to me to be a swirling porridge of patterns and colour, trying to conjure up the picture of leaping dolphins my son assured me was there all the time. "You aren't looking at it the right way. You need special vision," he reassured me. But I couldn't see anything at first except perhaps an Emperor's New Suit of Clothes, squinting and laughing back at me from the gift shop on the quayside. Once the picture finally shimmered into view though, it stayed for a long time. It was difficult to believe I couldn't see it in the first place, a beautiful collage of colour and light with three silver-blue dolphins dancing in a palpitating sea.

Ironically, this book is driven predominantly by a 'special' vision and is quite an eclectic mix of ideas and information drawn from all sorts of sometimes 'unlikely' sources. Malet Lambert School Language College has, as its mission statement, "We believe in 100% success for all", a statement of intent which was written to underpin a quite radical vision for raising standards in both the school and its wider community. The principle thrust of this vision has been to examine the nature and characteristics of effective learning in order that we might increase the motivation and efficacy of children in this process.

Some of the most inspirational areas of educational research in recent years have been in the development of strategies for improving thinking and learning and in the understanding of intelligence and cognitive neuroscience. Advances in cerebral imaging technology have allowed scientists to discover the biological processes that occur in the brain when human beings solve problems, act and think creatively, and make memories. It is now possible to understand more completely what kinds of conditions in the classroom are likely to produce successful learning, which preferred styles of learning children operate in and the 'brain-friendly' ways of accessing and developing different forms of intelligence as they manifest in the various talents youngsters display. The recently published National Curriculum 'Citizenship' orders (*Excellence in Schools*, DfES/QCA 1999) stress that children should "use their imaginations to consider other people's experiences and be able to think about, express and explain views that are not their own" (KS3: Developing skills of participation and responsible action). In other words, children should have the crucial interpersonal skill of empathy that features prominently in emotional intelligence.

Much of this vital information has been translated into the 'Learning to Learn' curriculum presented here. Through it, children will be taught motivational strategies such as making affirmations for success, risk-taking and comfort zones, anchoring positive states of mind using Neuro-Linguistic Programming (NLP) techniques, benchmarking successful people and emotional intelligence. They will explore the theories of Professor Howard Gardner on multiple intelligences and, using a specially written computer programme, learn about their own intelligence profile and preferred learning style based on visual, auditory and kinesthetic modes of representation. They will also learn about the most divinely complex organism in the universe, the human brain. All of these concepts and information will challenge children to think and then reflect metacognitively on the processes they themselves use when faced with new learning situations.

The most important aspect of 'Learning to Learn' is how well children understand the significance of *transferring* how and what they have learnt into different contexts. Knowing, for example, that you possess strong musical intelligence is of little consequence unless you know how to *utilise* that strength to learn effectively in other areas. Opportunities for transfer and generalisation are suggested in the lesson guidance for each chapter, as is the importance of the plenary in mediating this. The empowering of children with knowledge about this process and the theoretical foundation that underpins it can result in the creation of a dynamic dialogue about learning on a far more sophisticated level than might previously have been possible, as well as giving responsibility for the management of 'own learning' firmly back to the learner.

A model for planning lessons that works consistently with these theories is described later in this chapter through a template for an 'Effective Learning Structure'. This is just one model that follows a pattern for learning and review, which I feel is crucial to the assimilation and transfer of new knowledge and skills (an issue which, in itself, could be the subject of a fascinating book). I hope colleagues will experiment with its usage in subject areas as well in the planning of their own 'Learning to Learn' lessons.

In UK schools threshold assessment and performance management do make accountability for effective learning and pupil progress a crucial issue, and appropriate professional development for staff is an essential element of the course's successful delivery.

Learning to Learn, Citizenship and 'Inclusion'

Much of the DfES/QCA guidance on inclusion points to the application of Learning to Learn concepts in order to achieve successful and well-differentiated learning in classrooms. Examples cited in these orders include:

B. Responding to pupils' diverse learning needs (P.18–21)

3a   Creating effective learning environments

3b   Securing motivation and concentration *including* using teaching approaches appropriate to different learning styles and varying subject content and presentation so that it matches different learning needs

3c   Providing equality of opportunity through teaching approaches

3d   Setting targets for learning, including 'help pupils develop self-esteem and confidence in their ability to learn'.

(National Curriculum 'Citizenship' orders, *Excellence in Schools*,
DfES/QCA 1999, 'Inclusion', Sections 3a–3d)

Colleagues who are interested in pursuing research into new developments in learning research might contact Bill Lucas or Toby Greany at the Campaign for Learning, or any of the twenty-four CFL schools nationally which are involved in piloting strategies aimed at validating accelerated learning approaches. Early results processed by MORI on 'Learning to Learn in Schools', the three-year pilot study, show high levels of motivation and improved attainment in schools where these approaches are used and, in qualitative terms, a huge strengthening of pupils' versatility as learners. I would recommend Bill Lucas's excellent book *Power Up Your Mind* to all educationalists as it represents for me the kind of rational and discerning insight I seek most in my own research.

I was most keen that this book should *not do* two things:

First, that it should not be a self-proclaimed quick-fix programme for all – a kind of 'E's to A's overnight' panacea, full of preposterous and exaggerated claims that ultimately serve merely to trivialise serious academic research.

Second, that it should not be followed blindly. I intend that it be written (and received) in the spirit of excited but cautious enquiry. I have developed this 'Learning to Learn' curriculum over many years with the help of feedback from many staff and pupils, most of which has been very kind and supportive, though I am certain that the many talented and creative teachers who customise, adapt and embellish these lessons will, quite appropriately, personalise them in order to address the needs of the pupils they teach. I am also aware that there are probably many other things I could have included that are perfectly relevant to this field of study and would yield an equally productive Learning to Learn experience. But this foundation course is a selection of ideas and materials that seem to me to make a coherent and interesting programme for colleagues to teach and for children to enjoy learning from. Being an English teacher I have inevitably chosen many examples and illustrations from narrative, poetry, language and literacy and I realise that for some people this might represent a limitation or even an irritation. But I do believe that the examples are good ones and that children will enjoy reading them and completing the activities in order to assimilate the concepts, skills and knowledge that they teach.

Immediate, positive, success-affirming prose feedback on all that the children write, say and do in these lessons is part of the magic required to inspire and transform self-esteem and aspirations. As children reach a developmental stage where image and personal identity seem to matter more to them than material rewards, idiosyncratic praise for their achievements through feedback becomes even more crucial to their developing sense of self and in turn self-esteem. Advice for follow-up and feedback on the learning-styles questionnaire is also an important feature of the CD programme.

'Learning to Learn' is, I suppose, in essence exploring aspects of self-'hood' that in turn introduce new ways of looking at learning, new ways of responding and assimilating, new ways of accommodating and being flexible with information, new ways of perception and representation. And although this book does not pretend to offer any more than just ways to make a good start in this process, I hope that these are ways that, like those Magic Eye kaleidoscope collages, will only need to be glimpsed once before learning, achievement and aspiration are never quite the same again.

Garry Burnett, Advanced Skills Teacher, Malet Lambert School, Hull

Purpose of the Course: Objectives

Pupils will:

1. develop a positive attitude to learning and be encouraged to believe that they can be successful;

2. develop high self-esteem and self-worth and learn how to relate this to target-setting and affirmations;

3. develop thinking skills and demonstrate how these can be transferred across the curriculum;

4. identify their own learning style and illustrate how new ideas can be explored to cater for this individual learning style;

5. gain knowledge of some of the latest research into the function of the brain in learning and how to work, where possible, with the brain's most natural style of learning;

6. understand the concept of 'multiple intelligences' and how to work with a multi-modal approach to learning new information and skills;

7. become more skilled and resourceful at learning independently in any situation;
8. learn effective ways to improve memory and recall;

9. learn strategies to make learning more effective;

10. learn strategies to make learning more fun.

Planning for Effective Learning

The following template is a suggested model for planning lessons in an effective structure which supports the 'brain-friendly' theoretical foundation for the materials presented.

I am indebted to the work of Colin Rose, Mark Lovatt and Alistair Smith for the ideas that led me to devise this structure and I hope that colleagues might see the potential for using this in all areas of short-term planning.

Class Date Period	# An Effective Learning Structure
Predisposition The right environment	Aim to greet children with a welcoming and supportive environment as they arrive at the classroom. Displays should be relevant, recent, readable and interesting. *Smile*, using first names and, if appropriate, humour to reassure and help set a relaxing and convivial mood. Possibly use music to create ambience, to relate a positive mood and to connect to aspects of the topic. Dispel 'reptilian' brain states involved in the transition to a new environment. Arrange furniture appropriately – think carefully about composition of working groups, think about room ventilation or warmth, the need for natural light, sense of well-being, state of relaxed alertness, etc.
Context Connect the learning	A 2/3 minute 'settling-in' activity to re-fire the neural networks that host the information or skills being assimilated. For example: 1. Formulate three questions about the topic so far/previous lesson that can be answered with '*Yes*'. 2. Formulate three questions about the topic that can be answered with '*No*'. 3. Quick quiz (pupils test you?) etc. *No class register yet!*
Share objective(s) The big picture	Within *5 minutes* of the start of the lesson: Make sure the *learning objective* (possibly taken from programmes of study/levels) is already written clearly on the board (non-cursive text) and all irrelevant work from previous lessons wiped off. Discuss the vocabulary of the learning objective, the context and position of this lesson in the scheme of work. Describe the objective's link to the activity and how you perceive the activity might help pupils to complete the lesson objective. What will they know, understand or be able to do by the end of the lesson? Or how much nearer to this will they be?
Stimulus (VAK)	Introduce new information, *stimulus*, hook: **V**isual (video, picture, diagram, powerpoint, photograph, etc.) **A**uditory (tape, discussion, reading, etc.) **K**inesthetic (movement, artefact, physical activity, etc.)
Activity (Making meaning through Multiple Intelligences)	Should offer *challenge*, be *fun*, be well *paced* (time-bound), involve '*recencies*' (alternatives). Make use of Multiple Intelligence representations: Interpersonal Naturalist Intrapersonal Existentialist Linguistic Bodily-Kinesthetic Musical Visual Logical/Mathematical Suggest *extension* work/set homework.
Show you know	How will students demonstrate learning has taken place? Feedback to class, written work, pictorial representation, log, quiz, performance, 'each one teach one' (teach someone else) etc.
Plenary Mediation, transfer & generalisation	*Crucial – the 'process' must be mediated!* Return to the objective of the lesson. Share *feedback* on the learning. What *kinds* of thinking were used (hypothesising, categorisation, comparison, contrast, analogous thinking etc.)? Formulate questions to elicit metacognitive processes. Talk about *transferability* and the flexible application of this new information to other contexts. Draw out of pupils the relevance of what they have learnt to other areas of study. How does this *relate* to what they have already learnt? How *was it* learnt? In what ways might they think differently now? How has their understanding changed as a result of this new information? Encourage pupils to *generalise* its usage. Conclusion: *Preview* next lesson (headlines only). *Congratulate* class/pupils who have done particularly well, being specific about what you praise. Manage an orderly, considerate and systematic *departure* from the room.

Class Date Period	**Learning Plan**
Predisposition The right environment	
Context Connect the learning	
Share objective(s) The big picture	
Stimulus (VAK)	
Activity (Making meaning through Multiple Intelligences) Teacher offers 'mediation'	
Show you know	
Plenary Mediation, transfer & generalisation	

This page can be photocopied

'Learning to Learn – Making Learning Work'
Lesson Guidelines

These broad guidelines are meant to give the 'big picture' of the concepts and principles behind each of the sections and resources contained herein. As suggested in the 'Planning for Effective Learning' model, staff may wish to offer other kinds of stimulus (to address other intelligences and engage learning styles) and be selective about which of the resources they choose and how long they spend with their class on them. Other resources such as tapes, videos, DVDs, websites etc. can of course be introduced at the teacher's discretion. In particular I would like to draw attention to the excellent **CHAMPS** website (please see www.learntolearn.org for further details) which provides materials and activities that support the learning objectives presented here and provides extension and enrichment activities in a highly accessible way. The particular areas of the site are referenced at the end of each of these lesson guidelines. However colleagues choose to plan their Learning to Learn lessons, I would encourage a period of reflection during the plenary session when students should be invited to verbalise and re-contextualise what and how they have learned.

1. It's All in the Mind

Learning Objective

To develop a positive attitude to learning and be encouraged to believe one can be successful.

The main objective of this first section is to introduce the idea of motivation and to examine how we can separate different kinds of motivation into 'intrinsic' and 'extrinsic' forms. By introducing the course with **The Big Picture** it might be beneficial to talk about what kind of expectations students have of the course and to discuss *'What's in it for me?'*. The story **'The Mile'** details how a young boy who has been bullied decides to fight back in a non-violent way. His motivation is pride, not material success and interesting discussions about why he actually walks off the track at the end of the story might follow. The **Peter Pan** and **Magic Moments** exercises are to show the importance of positive thinking (a theme which will be referred to throughout the first section). **Magic Moments** could even be the subject of a homework or extension (this has been used as a cross-phase transfer/induction day activity). Children should bring in their decorated envelopes and mementoes in order to share some of their positive memories and achievements.

See also CHAMPS   Confident to Learn   *'Believe in Yourself'*

2. *Looking Forward*

Learning Objective

To develop a very positive view of the future and the ability to make plans for change

The exercises in this section begin with **'A Chronicle of the Future'**, which offers students an opportunity to describe a very positive personal vision of the future. Introductory discussion might cover the way that science fiction has contributed to 'inventing' the future (*Star Trek*, for example, and the mobile phone). The point is, of course, that we wish to stress that human beings are capable of creating and sustaining visions of themselves as something that, in current reality, doesn't yet exist. This can be reinforced by the **Epitaph** exercise which invites students to project a vision of their own future achievements. Invite students to think about the awful scenario of missing a whole period of your life (coma or accident etc.). Talk about people who have had a vision of themselves in the future and have subsequently made huge changes to the way they behave (Ebeneezer Scrooge, Macbeth etc.). **Start Dreaming!** and **What am I Most Looking Forward to?** are meant to reinforce the idea that 'inventing' the future depends on the vision of the individual. **Potential** introduces the idea that 'success' depends so much on releasing hidden talents and acknowledging that within every human being lies a 'sleeping giant'. **School Reunion**, like **Epitaph**, invites students to project a vision of themselves in the future at an imaginary get-together of their peers.

See also CHAMPS   Confident to Learn   *'Believe in Yourself'*

3. *If You Always Do …*

Learning Objective

To learn how to feel confident taking risks and stepping outside of one's comfort zone to make positive change

Comfort Zones and Risk are concepts which children need to explore in order to be equipped to challenge the routines and patterns in their lives that yield them little in terms of personal growth. This is not to undermine the need that people have for order and 'stability' in their lives, but reflects the idea that 'cognitive conflict' can cause human beings to be very creative in trying to achieve resolution. To wilfully throw your system out of order and confront fear and insecurity can lead to increased personal confidence and inner strength. The story of **'Jack and the Storytelling Contest'** introduces the idea of how it might be possible to be trapped in a comfort zone and therefore be incapable of coping with life-changing, dramatic alterations to personal circumstances. How do we cope with change? Do we ever challenge what we hold dear? Are we prepared to take the risks which might make the difference to the way we think and act in the future? **'Between the Lights'** describes reminiscences of childhood fears and 'running away' to try to solve them. Until the fear is actually confronted head on, no positive, affective change is made. Encourage pupils to transfer and think about the challenges ahead – examinations, careers, higher education, etc. Cultivate positive and optimistic attitudes to taking risks and confronting fear.

See also CHAMPS   Confident to Learn   *'Sit back and think' – whole section*
    'Push your comfort zones'
    'Reflect on it '

4. Think You Can

Learning Objective

Know how to create and sustain a positive state of mind to take on
new challenges in learning

This section explores the need for 'positive focus' to achieve. *The Empire Strikes Back* extract – **Luke Trains to be a Jedi** (which might also be shown on video to enhance the message) explores the idea that focused meditation on a positive outcome can lead to more determined aspiration to achieve a goal. Many children with low self-esteem give up easily when confronted with setbacks. This section is designed to introduce 'tenacity' through engineering a positive and sustained focus on achievement. **'If'** and **Slogans for Success** offer different interpretations of this same principle with visual and linguistic activities to differentiate them.

See also CHAMPS   'Confident to Learn'   *'Believe in Yourself'*

5. Mission Impossible?

Learning Objective

Know how to create and sustain a positive state of mind to take on
new challenges in learning

This section is designed to confront the low expectations and aspirations which dog under-achievement. **The Story of the Four-Minute Mile** and **The Remarkable Story of Cliff Young** are similar tales of male athletes, but the most remarkable thing about both tales is that the year after these new records were set, many other people were able to achieve even more astonishing times.

State of mind and self-belief was clearly an influencing factor.

Teachers should stress in these lessons that ceilings of achievement are often self-inflicted barriers and that to liberate our self-imposed restrictions through zero tolerance of failure (failure is just a setback) allows us to tap a much bigger barrel of success.

'It Couldn't be Done!' and **Join the Dots** make this same point in different ways. (The solutions to these problems, by the way, can be found on the Malet Lambert School website.)

See also CHAMPS   'Confident to Learn'   *'Believe in Yourself'*

6. Affirmations

Learning Objective

To use the technique of making affirmations to reinforce positive and ambitious target-setting

On New Year's Day the gym I attend is crowded with people who have made drastic resolutions to lose weight and get fit. **Turning Goals into Affirmations** is meant to show the power of the mind to *visualise* a new 'self', to have a very strong positive image of the future self as somebody different, more motivated and goal-centred. Drawing on the work of Lou Tice and the Pacific Institute on 'teleological' thinking this section aims to affect thinking about what people 'want to be' in order to direct them towards being more capable, confident and resolved. Examples of achievers who have been single-minded about their goals are cited, but especially **Tiger Woods – Born to Reign** who famously wrote down his very powerful affirmations for success.

The difference between affirmations and resolutions (the reason why the gym is half-empty again by the end of January) is challenged in **Wannabes and Affirmations**, which explores the need for what Lou Tice calls 'cognitive dissonance' (the energising difference here between the self *now* and a future projection of the self). Writing **Affirmations** and **Making the Affirmation SMART** leads children through the process of writing out goals in a way which is affective and motivational to change.

See also CHAMPS   'Confident to Learn'   *'Programme Yourself'*

7. Food for Thought

Learning Objective

To use the technique of making affirmations to reinforce positive and ambitious target-setting

Musical Affirmations consolidates the work on linguistic affirmations by introducing a different representational form of the affirmation, the lyric or anthem. Children should be encouraged to write, perform, play their own motivational songs and to explain why they find that song or tune inspirational. Parents and teachers might also contribute 'Our Tunes', songs that have become soundtracks to emotional high or low points in their lives. **'Moonshadow', 'Something**

Inside (So strong)' and 'The Greatest Love of All' are only three personal favourites, but I'm sure students and teachers will assemble quite a collection of personal motivational songs and tunes.

See also CHAMPS   'Confident to Learn'   *'Programme Yourself'*

8. Inspiration …

Learning Objective

To learn how to benchmark people who have already been successful in areas
where I want to grow and change

The linking feature of these three activities is the utilisation of models of success to anchor in the mind states of positive, inspirational thinking. **Benchmarking Success** invites children to correspond with mentors and idols, to research the methods and thinking which informs their success. Building this understanding can lead to these associations being drawn upon to suggest images of success and positive feeling and to connect with the task ahead. The ideas for such 'modelling' are based on very powerful **'Neuro-Linguistic Programming'** techniques for 'anchoring' positive states of mind and dispelling reptilian brain states. In order to help focus and associate positive thoughts **'The Impossible Dream'** song lyrics and **'Anchors Aweigh!'** activities offer musical and kinesthetic alternatives.

9. Emotional Intelligence

Learning Objective

To understand that through 'emotional' intelligence we can be more positive and effective as
learners and understand the needs of others

The main objective of gaining an understanding of 'emotional' intelligence is to increase sensitivity to the needs of others and awareness of the complex emotional responses we make to different situations. We have already explored 'tenacity' and resilience to 'failure' (we should try to view 'failure' as a setback). Here we look at other aspects of 'personal' intelligences defined by Daniel Goleman as a crucial attribute to enable us to sustain motivation, work in harmony and to respect the emotional complexity of our selves and others. **'Terry Dobson and the Japanese Drunk'** illustrates how impulsive, aggressive responses to aggression are not always the ideal solutions to confrontational situations. **A Yuletide Tale** (see also CD version) is a story about a boy being teased for crying. How often do children scoff at the emotional responses others make (especially boys)? The story is meant to help surface attitudes to showing emotion, responding impulsively and acknowledging the varied emotional responses we have to control. **'Still I rise'** by Maya Angelou is a poetic account of courage to remain strong, tenacious and alive in the face of overwhelming set-backs, a valued trait of emotional intelligence.

10. Evaluation and Transfer

Learning Objective

Evaluation and transfer to encourage reflection, discussion and the transferability of all that they have covered in Learning to Learn

See also CHAMPS   'Sit back and think'   *Whole section*

11. A Cage With Stout Bars?

Learning Objective(s)

To understand that different kinds of learning might require different cognitive strategies
To understand that the environment and 'teaching' of new information and skills can affect the success of the learning

The Red Cockatoo and **Kinds of Learning: 'KUS'** introduce discussion and thinking about aspects of teaching and learning. This section is meant to encourage reflection on positive and negative school experiences as well as to engage in the categorisation of different learning situations. The point of this is to encourage children to reflect on the different cognitive strategies required to learn successfully (memory, understanding, skill etc.) leading to future work on thinking skill acquisition and development. **Mr Gorman** (see also CD version) or **Miss Creedle** are two accounts of questionable 'teaching' methodology. Can students unpick from these examples the qualities which make learning successful or unsuccessful? The application of this in 'transfer' is to how they can then manufacture learning situations for themselves, leading to an understanding of preferred learning styles and multiple intelligence theory.

See also CHAMPS   'Introduction'   *'What will CHAMPS do for you?*
'The best techniques for you'

12. Your Remarkable Brain

Learning Objective

To gain knowledge of some of the latest research into the brain and how to work with the brain's most natural style of learning

The crucial reason for studying different operational qualities of the brain in this context is to understand its capacity and function for learning and to adapt some of that understanding into methods for creating conditions for effective learning.

Students will learn facts about the brain, including information about the 'tri-une model', the recticular formation and the importance of making connections. In order to put some of this information into practice they will learn about Tony Buzan's technique of 'Mindmapping' (see also the video clip).

See also CHAMPS	'Introduction	*'Your brilliant brain'*
	'Confident to learn	*'Fit to learn'*
	'Home in on the facts'	*'What's the big idea?'*

13. Multiple Intelligences and Learning Styles

Learning Objective(s)

To understand more about the style of learning I prefer
To understand how to recognise and use different kinds of intelligence to learn

Five things About Me is a useful way to introduce this section as it offers the opportunity to discuss the varied and unique profile of ability, experience and interests that lie within a single group of people. This is to lead to an exploration of varied and unique combinations of intelligence that exist within ourselves and within the class. I thought it might be useful to consider different manifestations of intelligence in fictional, historical and anomalous representations in order to try to rationalise how we perceive and define intelligence. **Intelligence, Run, Forrest; Blind Tom** etc. depict factual and fictional characters who have displayed enormous qualities of intelligence in quite varied fields. Howard Gardner's work on **Multiple Intelligences** is introduced with a view to children understanding that their IQ' should be a reflection of their ability to perceive and represent the world in a variety of contexts (not just word and number). **VAK Learning in Style** is to lead children to understanding that a preferred learning style is the ability to flexibly adapt to any new learning situation and not to be 'stuck' for a way of learning something new. Students should also complete their own learning profile (see the 2 CD programmes).

See also CHAMPS	'Home in on the Facts'	*Whole section*
	'Action'	*Whole section*

14. *Learning to Learn*

Learning Objective(s)

To develop strategies for improving recall
To become skilled and resourceful at applying knowledge gained through
Learning to Learn to practical situations

This final section sees the application of several **Memory** techniques to practical learning situations. **'He who has learned to learn'** from Guy Claxton illustrates a master learner at work. **Chunking, Association** and **Mnemonics** introduces three strategies which can be re-applied to different learning situations especially **SpellCAM**, which sees the application of these three particular strategies to an aspect of literacy. Having a good memory on its own is not regarded as evidence of high intelligence (witness the echolalic ability of the savant) despite it being an important quality of learning. *Flexibility* in the way we use information is witness to the ability to transfer recall into understanding.

The plenary session is crucial in mediating this process and should be emphasised in the teaching of all thinking and memory skills.

See also CHAMPS   'Memorise it'   *Whole section*

15. *Evaluation and Review*

Evaluation and review encourage reflection, discussion and the transferability of all they have covered in Learning to Learn into other contexts.

See also CHAMPS   'Sit back and Think'   *Whole section*

Effective Learning: Thinking You Can

Chapter One
It's All in the Mind

Learning to Learn: The Big Picture

The purpose of this course is to help you gain learning super-fitness. We want to improve your ability to learn in any new situation and for you to feel confident and motivated to achieve this. The activities and materials included here are designed to make you think about the *way* you think and learn. As you look back on each of these lessons, try to see how you could use what you have learnt in other learning situations. This is called 'transfer' and your teacher will be seeking ways to help you understand the importance of this process.

During this course you will learn about:

- Motivation
- Thinking positively
- Breaking down barriers to achievement
- Thinking *you can*
- Comfort zones – how to expand your mind and your confidence
- Making affirmations for success
- Using music and movement to help anchor positive states of mind
- Benchmarking successful people
- Finding inspiration
- Tenacity – not giving up
- How to use your brain power to learn and remember more effectively
- How to build a healthier learning brain
- Improving strategies for memory
- Mindmapping
- Types of intelligence
- Understanding your own learning style

Have fun and enjoy 'Learning to Learn'.

Kinds of Motivation: Intrinsic and Extrinsic

Some things we have to do. Some things we are expected to do. Some things we are told to do. Being 'motivated' means *wanting* to do something. People are often more motivated when they receive some kind of reward. Sometimes, the reason people have for doing something is to achieve their own satisfaction or pleasure. Lots of people have hobbies and interests that they do with great dedication even though no one has asked or told them to.

Think of times when you have been rewarded in some way for what you have done. The reward could have been a certificate, a prize, a sweet or even money! It could have been your own pleasure or the receipt of praise from someone you respect. In other words, what do you get out of it? An important motivating state of mind is when you realise 'what's in it for you', what you will get out of it personally, or in terms of a material reward. *Motivation* might be categorised broadly in the following ways:

Intrinsic   where the reason you have to do your best is inside, it is for you.
Extrinsic   where the reason is 'material' or outside, it is for the prize or reward.

Discuss some of the following situations. What motivates you?

- Playing for a school team
- Doing your hobby (dancing, sport, drama, collecting etc.)
- Doing your homework
- Helping out in the home (doing dishes, tidying up, doing errands etc.)
- Watching your favourite programme on the television
- Beating your best score on your computer game
- Doing your paper round or a job to earn pocket money

Is the motivation in each of these cases intrinsic or extrinsic? Or possibly both?
Make a list of different things you do in a typical week and decide whether they are extrinsically or intrinsically motivated.

Task/activity	Extrinsic	Intrinsic

Who Wants to be a Millionaire?

"Hi, my name is Garrison Burns, trillionaire Internet businessman. Some say I am 'eccentric'; I prefer to say 'public spirited'. I am willing to offer the sum of £1,000,000 to any student who will guarantee to get 10 GCSE passes at grade C and above. No catches, just write to me pledging that you will undertake to do this and telling me how you will achieve it. So come on, who wants to be a millionaire?"

Suppose this was a genuine offer. How many of us would suddenly find the motivation to be able to achieve it? Yet the average person who achieves good qualifications in a 40-year working life will often earn far in excess of this amount.

I could easily have changed the offer to 'Who can: run a marathon in under three hours; climb to the top of Everest; learn to read; play the mandolin; learn to speak Chinese etc.'

We all live privileged lives full of opportunity. If our motives are deeper and more personal then we need 'material' incentive less and less. Mozart and Van Gogh, two of the greatest artists that ever lived, both died in poverty, ignored and lonely. Yet they continued to work and to produce magnificent art to the end of their sad lives, driven by an intrinsic motivation to create and to produce beautiful works of music and art.

In many ways intrinsic motivation is far more powerful than motivation that is driven by any kind of material reward. Intrinsically motivated people only rely on themselves for inspiration (see the lyrics to the song '**The Greatest Love of All**'). *So how do we create it?*

Read the following story about 'motivation', then answer the questions and try the activities that follow.

The Mile

What a rotten report. It was the worst report I'd ever had. I'd dreaded bringing it home for my mum to read. We were sitting at the kitchen table having our tea, but neither of us had touched anything. It was gammon and chips as well, with a pineapple ring. My favourite. We have gammon every Friday, because my Auntie Doreen works on the bacon counter at the Co-op, and she drops it in on her way home. I don't think she pays for it.

My mum was reading the report for the third time. She put it down on the table and stared at me. I didn't say anything. I just stared at my gammon and chips and pineapple ring. What could I say? My mum looked so disappointed. I really felt sorry for her. She was determined for me to do well at school, and get my 'A' Levels, then go to University, then get my degree, and then get a good job with good prospects.

"I'm sorry, Mum …"

She picked up the report again, and started reading it for the fourth time. "It's no good reading it again, Mum. It's not going to get any better."

She slammed the report back onto the table.

"Don't you make cheeky remarks to me. I'm not in the mood for it!"

I hadn't meant it to be cheeky but I suppose it came out like that.

"I wouldn't say anything if I was you, after reading this report!"

I shrugged my shoulders.

"There's nothing much I *can* say, is there?"

"You can tell me what went wrong. You told me you worked hard this term!"

I *had* told her I'd worked hard but I hadn't.

"I did work hard, Mum."

"Not according to this."

She waved the report under my nose.

"You're supposed to be taking your 'O' Levels next year. What do you think is going to happen then?"

I shrugged my shoulders again and stared at my gammon and chips.

"I don't know."

She put the report back on the table. I knew I hadn't done well in my exams because of everything that had happened this term, but I didn't think for a moment I'd come bottom in nearly everything. Even Norbert Lightowler had done better than me.

"You've come bottom in nearly everything. Listen to this."

She picked up the report again.

"Maths – Inattentive and lazy."

I knew what it said.

"I know what it says, Mum."

She leaned across the table, and put her face close to mine.

"I know what it says too, and I don't like it. I mean you didn't even do well at sport, did you? 'Sport – He is not a natural athlete.' Didn't you do *anything* right this term?"

I couldn't help smiling to myself. No, I'm not a natural athlete, but I'd done one thing right this term. I'd shown Arthur Boocock that he couldn't push me around any more. That's why everything else had gone wrong. That's why I was "lazy and inattentive" at Maths and "capricious and dilettantish" at English Language. That's why this last term had been so miserable, because of Arthur blooming Boocock.

He'd only come into our class this year because he'd been kept down. I didn't like him. He's a right bully, but because he's a bit older and is good at sport and running and things, everybody does what he says.

That's how Smokers' Corner started.

Arthur used to pinch his dad's cigarettes and bring them to school, and we'd smoke them at playtime in the shelter under the woodwork classroom. We called it Smokers' Corner. It was daft really. I didn't even like smoking, it gives me headaches. But I joined in because all the others did. Well I didn't want Arthur Boocock picking on me. We took it in turns to stand guard. I liked it when it was my turn, it meant I didn't have to join in the smoking.

Smokers' Corner was at the top end of the playground, opposite the girls' school. That's how I first saw Janis. It was one playtime. I was on guard when I saw these three girls staring at me from an upstairs window. They kept laughing and giggling. I didn't take much notice, which was a good job, because I saw Melrose coming across the playground with Mr Rushton, the Deputy Head. I ran into the shelter and warned the lads.

"Arthur, Tony – Melrose and Rushton are coming!"

There was no way we could've been caught. We knew we could get everything away before Melrose or Rushton or anybody could reach us, even if they ran across the playground as fast as they could. We had a plan you see.

First, everybody put their cigarettes out, but not on the ground, with your fingers. It didn't half hurt if you didn't wet them enough. Then Arthur would open a little iron door that was in the wall next to the boiler house. Norbert had found it ages ago. It must've been there for years. Tony reckoned it was some sort of oven. Anyway, we'd empty our pockets and put all the cigarettes inside. All the time we'd be waving our hands about to get rid of the smoke, and Arthur would squirt the fresh-air spray he'd nicked from home. Then we'd shut the iron door and start playing football or tig.

Melrose never let on why he used to come storming across the playground. He never said anything, but we knew he was trying to catch the Smokers, and he knew that we knew. All he'd do was give us all a look in turn, and march off. But on that day, the day those girls had been staring and giggling at me, he did say something.

"Watch it! All of you. I know what you're up to. Just watch it. Specially you, Boocock."

We knew why Melrose picked on Arthur Boocock.

"You're running for the school on Saturday, Boocock. You'd better win, or I'll want to know the reason why."

Mr Melrose is in charge of athletics, and Arthur holds the record for the mile. Melrose reckons he could run for Yorkshire one day if he trains hard enough.

I didn't like this smoking lark, it made me cough, gave me a headache, and I was sure we'd get caught one day.

"Hey, Arthur, we'd better pack it in. Melrose is going to catch us one of these days."

Arthur wasn't bothered.

"Ah you, you're just scared, you're yeller!"

Yeah, I was blooming scared.

"I'm not. I just think he's going to catch us."

Then Arthur did something that really shook me. He took his right hand out of his blazer pocket. For a minute I thought he was going to hit me, but he didn't. He put it to his mouth instead, and blew out some smoke. He's mad. I didn't say anything though. I was scared he'd thump me.

I often looked out for her after that, but when I saw her she was always with the other two. The one time I did see her on her own, I was walking home with Tony and Norbert and I pretended I didn't know her, even though she smiled and said hello. Of course, I sometimes used to see her at playtime, when it was my turn to stand guard at Smokers' Corner. I liked being on guard twice as much now. As well as not having to smoke, it gave me a chance to see Janis. She was smashing. I couldn't get her out of my mind. I was always thinking about her, you know, having daydreams when I heard Melrose shouting his head off.

"Straight to the Headmaster's study. Go on, all three of you!"

I looked round and I couldn't believe it. Melrose was inside Smokers' Corner. He'd caught Arthur, Tony and Norbert. He was giving Arthur a right crack over the head. How had he caught them? I'd been there all the time … standing guard … thinking about Janis … I just hadn't seen him coming … oh heck …

"I warned you, Boocock, all of you. Go and report to the Headmaster!"

As he was going past me, Arthur showed me his fist. I knew what that meant.

They all got the cane for smoking, and Melrose had it in for Arthur even though he was still doing well at his running. The more Melrose picked on Arthur, the worse it was for me because Arthur kept beating me up.

That was the first thing he'd done after he'd got the cane – beaten me up. He reckoned I'd not warned them about Melrose on purpose.

"How come you didn't see him? He's blooming big enough."

"I just didn't."

I couldn't tell him that I'd been dreaming about Janis Webster.

"He must've crept up behind me."

Arthur hit me, right on my ear.

"How could he go behind you? You had your back to the wall. You did it on purpose, you yeller-belly!"

And he hit me again, on the same ear.

After that, Arthur hit me every time he saw me. Sometimes, he'd hit me in the stomach, sometimes on the back of my neck. Sometimes, he'd raise his fist and I'd think he was going to hit me, and he'd just walk away, laughing. Then he started taking my spending money. He'd say, "Oh, you don't want that, do you?" and I'd say, "No, you have it, Arthur."

I was really scared of him. He made my life a misery. I dreaded going to school, and when I could, I'd stay at home by pretending to be poorly. I used to stick my fingers down my throat and make myself sick.

I suppose that's when I started to get behind with my school work, but anything was better than being bullied by that rotten Arthur Boocock. And when I did go to school, I'd try to stay in the classroom at playtime, or I'd make sure I was near the teacher who was on playground duty. Of course, Arthur thought it was all very funny, and he'd see if he could hit me without the teacher seeing, which he could.

Dinner time was the worst because we had an hour free before the bell went for school dinners, and no one was allowed to stay inside. It was a school rule. That was an hour for Arthur to bully me. I used to try to hide but he'd always find me.

By now it didn't seem to have anything to do with him being caught smoking and getting the cane. He just seemed to enjoy hitting me and tormenting me. So I stopped going to school dinners. I used to get some chips, or a Cornish pasty and wander around. Sometimes I'd go into town and look at the shops; or else I'd go in the park and muck about. Anything to get away from school and Arthur Boocock.

That's how I met Archie.

There's a running track in the park, a proper one with white lines and every-thing, and one day I spent all dinner time watching this old bloke running round and round and I got talking to him.

"Hey, mister, how fast can you run a mile?"

I was holding a bag of crisps, and he came over and took one. He grinned at me.

"How fast can *you* run a mile?"

I'd never tried running a mile.

"I don't know, I've never tried."

He grinned again.

"Well now's your chance. Come on, get your jacket off."

He was ever so fast and I found it hard to keep up with him, but he told me I'd done well. I used to run with Archie every day after that. He gave me an old tracksuit top, and I'd change into my shorts and trainers and chase round the track after him. Archie said I was getting better and better.

"You'll be running for Yorkshire one of these days."

I laughed and told him to stop teasing me. He gave me half an orange. He always did after running.

"Listen, lad, I'm serious. It's all a matter of training. Anybody can be good if they train hard enough. See you tomorrow."

That's when I got the idea.

I decided to go in for the mile in the school sports at the end of term. You had to be picked for everything else, but anybody could enter the mile. There were three weeks to the end of term, and in that three weeks I ran everywhere. I ran to school. I ran with Archie every dinner time. I went back and ran on the track after school. Then I'd run home. If my mum wanted anything from the shops, I'd run there. I'd get up really early in the mornings and run before breakfast. I was always running. I got into tons of trouble at school for not doing my homework properly, but I didn't care. All I thought about was the mile.

I had daydreams about it. Always me and Arthur, neck and neck, and Janis would be cheering me on.

Arthur did well at sports day. He won the high jump and the long jump. He was picked for the half-mile and the forty-four, and won them both. Then there was an announcement for the mile.

"Will all those competitors who want to enter the open mile please report to Mr Melrose at the start."

I hadn't let on to anybody that I was going to enter, so everyone was very surprised to see me when I went over in my shorts and trainers – especially Melrose. Arthur thought it was hilarious.

"Well, look who it is. Do you want me to give you half a mile start?"

I ignored him, and waited for Melrose to start the race.

I surprised a lot of people that day, but nobody more than Arthur. I stuck to him like a shadow. When he went forward, I went forward. If he dropped back, I dropped back. This went on for about half the race. He kept giving me funny looks. He couldn't understand what was happening.

"You won't keep this up. Just watch."

And he suddenly spurted forward. I followed him, and when he looked round to see how far ahead he was, he got a shock when he saw he wasn't.

It was just like my daydreams. Arthur and me, neck and neck, the whole school cheering us on, both of us heading for the last bend. I looked at Arthur and saw the tears rolling down his cheeks. He was crying his eyes out. I knew at that moment I'd beaten him. I don't mean I knew I'd won the race. I wasn't bothered about that. I knew I'd beaten *him, Arthur*. I knew he'd never hit me again.

That's when I walked off the track. I didn't see any point in running the last two hundred yards. I suppose that's because I'm not a natural athlete …

"'Sport – He is not a natural athlete.' Didn't you do *anything* right this term?"

Blimey! My mum was still reading my report. I started to eat my gammon and chips. They'd gone cold.

(George Layton, adapted from *A Northern Childhood – The Fib and other Stories*)

Follow-up activities
'Put-downs and put-ups'

Questions

1. What 'motivates' the boy to beat Arthur Boocock?
2. What are the things that make him feel bad about himself?
3. How does he cope with them?
4. What does Archie say that helps the boy?
5. Why do you think he walks off the track at the end of the story?
6. Who are the important people in your own life that help you to succeed?
7. What kinds of thing do they say to you that give you encouragement?

Activity

Turn the story of 'The Mile' into a class play. Perform it in an assembly or to a year lower than your own. Add music and movement. Alternatively, turn it into a radio play with music and sound effects. For an extra challenge, record it live. No stopping or pausing the tape recorder!

Try to get across the important message about being motivated and determined about achieving your goals.

Transfer

- What have you learnt about motivation from this story?
- What is your main kind of motivation in life? Try to monitor yourself. Ask "What's in it for me if I do this or that?" Sometimes the reward might not be immediate but rather much more long-term and valuable.

Peter Teaches the Children How to Fly

Read the following extract from the children's book *Peter Pan* by J. M. Barrie. Peter Pan has agreed to teach the children how to fly and insists that in order to do so you need to do something very special. Some people have seen this as a 'metaphor' (a way of explaining by comparison) for positive thinking.

"I can't fly."

"I'll teach you."

"Oh, how lovely to fly."

"I'll teach you how to jump on the wind's back, and then away we go."

"Oo," and her arms went out to him.

How could she resist. "Of course it's awfully fascinating!" she cried. "Peter, would you teach John and Michael to fly too?"

"If you like," he said indifferently, and she ran to John and Michael and shook them. "Wake up," she cried, "Peter Pan has come and he is to teach us to fly."

"I say, Peter, can you really fly?"

Instead of troubling to answer him Peter flew around the room, taking the mantelpiece on the way.

"How topping!" said John and Michael.

"How sweet!" cried Wendy.

It looked delightfully easy, and they tried it first from the floor and then from the beds, but they always went down instead of up.

"I say, how do you do it?" asked John, rubbing his knee. He was quite a practical boy.

"You just think lovely wonderful thoughts," Peter explained, "and they lift you up in the air."

He showed them again.

(J. M. Barrie, from *Peter Pan*)

Discuss

How do you think needing to have a happy thought to fly is like being in the right state of mind for learning?

Magic Moments ...

"If I keep a green bough in my heart, a bird will come to sing"
(Chinese proverb)

One of the most moving scenes in the film *Billy Elliot* is when Billy (played by Jamie Bell) is about to take dancing up seriously. His teacher (played by Julie Walters) invites him to bring along a collection of things, including a letter from his dead mother, that will make him *feel good* about himself. His collection is a small treasure chest of possessions that help to conjure up happy and positive feelings. His teacher knows he will then 'connect' these happy and positive feelings with his dancing lessons.

We all have times that we like to look back on and remember fondly. Many of us keep photographs and certificates, 'memorabilia' such as concert programmes and postcards to remind us of happy times.

Have you noticed how just looking at these mementoes can bring back a flood of positive memories and positive feelings? They make us *feel good*.

We want you to bring this '*feel-good*' factor to learning.

Activity 1

Think about a time you did something that you were really proud of or that made you happy.

You may be thinking of a time when you needed to show courage; it might be when you stood up for yourself against someone who was being loud and unfriendly or when you had to go in front of a large group of people and speak or read aloud. It could be a time when you won a prize for some personal achievement, a family celebration such as a party or get-together or maybe an occasion on which you were praised for doing something really well. Maybe you are thinking of a family holiday or day out, a visit to a concert or the theatre or a school trip.

Discuss this with a partner.

Your teacher may ask one or two people to share their 'magic moments' with the class.

Activity 2

Choose three of your favourite personal 'magic moments' and write a brief description of the times they happened. Try to describe exactly what happened, the sights (colours and surroundings), sounds and feelings you remember.

Use this writing frame to help you:

One of my 'magic moments' was when ...

It made me feel ...

Another 'magic moment' was when ...

This made me feel ...

One final 'magic moment' was when ...

I felt ...

Homework/Extension

Collect together a *'Magic Moments'* personal file: Decorate a large A4 envelope and place in it a selection of these 'magic moments' mementoes ready to bring to your first 'Learning to Learn' lessons.

Use these to help link positive feelings to whatever new and challenging task you have to do.

Chapter Two

Looking Forward

A Chronicle of the Future

Think of some of the many films and TV programmes that have been set in the future (*Star Wars, Star Trek, Deep Space Nine* etc.).

Discuss how the future is represented in the media and in books you have read. Do they portray it as a time to look forward to? How?

Read the following predictions made by scientists about what the future might hold:

Human beings will begin genetic experiments which will give them the abilities only held by animals, for example the sense of smell of a dog, the eyesight of a hawk etc. One day we will be able to tap into the part of the brain where we fantasise and project the images onto a screen. Those who have the most vivid and imaginative fantasies will be the film-makers of the future.

Diseases and infections will be a rare thing, and all of the major illnesses we currently die from will have cures found for them.

(From 'A Chronicle of the Future', the *Sunday Times* 29th April, 1999)

Transfer

Think carefully about your own future. How much of your future can be invented? (The answer is, practically all of it.) You are the 'captain' of your destiny. You decide the area you would like to grow strong in.

Activities

1. Write a short press release or news broadcast about an exciting new discovery or invention (*250 words max*). Begin it with: "Scientists have released details today of a remarkable new _____ that will revolutionise all of our lives ..."
2. Draw or design the invention you would like to see happen. Put in as much detail as you can. Don't worry about 'how' it will happen – one hundred years ago many of the things we take for granted today were merely ideas or dreams.

Epitaph

Three friends die in a car accident and they go to a meeting in heaven. They are all asked, "When you are in your coffin and friends and family are mourning you, what would you like to hear them say about you?"

The first man says, "I would like to hear them say that I was a great doctor of my time, and a great family man."

The second man says, "I would like to hear that I was a wonderful husband and school teacher who made a huge difference to the children of tomorrow."

The last man replies, "I would like to hear them say ... LOOK, HE'S MOVING!!!!!!!!!!!!!"

Questions and activity

1. It is perhaps a morbid thought, but how would you like to be remembered?
2. What kind of things would you like to achieve in your lifetime?
3. Make a list of lifetime goals – things to look forward to.

Start Dreaming!

Pure Imagination

Come with me and you'll be
In a world of pure imagination
Take a look and you'll see
Into your imagination

We'll begin with a spin
Trav'ling in the world of my creation
What we'll see will defy
Explanation

If you want to view paradise
Simply look around and view it
Anything you want to, do it
Want to change the world, there's nothing to it

There is no life I know
To compare with pure imagination
Living there, you'll be free
If you truly wish to be

(From *Willy Wonka and the Chocolate Factory*)

If you believe that the future is there for you to invent, you will start to believe in your own very powerful ability to control your life – to be assertive and to make decisions about facing up to the things that hold you back or make you feel afraid.

Through the work you do in 'Learning to Learn' you will begin to believe that you have the potential to achieve great things in your life and to learn in a style that suits you with confidence and self-esteem.

So start dreaming! What do you want to achieve in your education and in your life? The only thing that's stopping you *is* you! Complete the following sheet: 'What am I Most Looking Forward to?' and then we can begin the process of building the state of mind and attitude that will help you achieve these things.

What am I Most Looking Forward to?

Everyone 'looks forward' to something in the future; holidays, Christmas, birthdays, a special day out or an event. They try to imagine what the experience will be like and it gives them pleasure and motivation. Looking 'forward' is an important ingredient of goal-setting.

What am I most looking forward to:

In life?

_____

_____

_____

_____

_____

In my family?

_____

_____

_____

_____

_____

At school?

_____

_____

_____

_____

_____

In my career?

_____

_____

_____

_____

_____

Potential

"You are your potential, not your past"

In January 1992, our local commercial radio station, Viking FM, invited Malet Lambert School, Hull, to host an up-and-coming pop group to perform songs from their new album to a lunch-time crowd of pupils and teachers.

At the time I ran *ETC*, the school magazine, and we were invited to interview the group and write an article on them. "Just another pretty boy-band," I thought, "another flash-in-the-pan, record-company-hyped, pretty boy-band," as they bounded up the stairs to the room backstage where the interviews would be held.

Image aside, they were a surprisingly nice, intelligent group of blokes, aware that they probably had only a couple of years' 'shelf-life' before they disappeared into obscurity. They were all immaculately groomed – hair, clothes and shoes – and they all ate and drank very carefully in order to preserve their sylph-like figures.

All except one. He looked a little scruffier than the rest, wore a checked lumber-jacket and kept making (sometimes funny) jokes about himself and the band. It was as if he felt uncomfortable being where he was and doing what he was doing and I thought, if anything, he could possibly be a liability to them and hamper their chances of future success.

The school hall was packed with screaming girls and boys as the band pranced and preened through their twenty-minute routine but, like many of the other staff, I wasn't overly keen. In fact it all seemed quite funny at the time.

The last thing I remember saying to the band as they got changed in the tiny room that is now my office was, "Good luck, lads," but I remember thinking "That's the last I'll see of them!" as they drove out of the school playground in a hired minibus while two girls from another school banged on its side.

Well so I thought.

Earlier this month, I took my own children to see the so-called scruffy misfit perform to over 60,000 people at the Millennium Stadium in Cardiff. It was one of the best live concerts I have ever seen and I thoroughly enjoyed singing and dancing along to the songs with the rest of the crowd. I had failed to spot his potential. So, by the sound of it, did the rest of the group.

You see the group that visited us that day was called Take That and the scruffy lad whose potential was, at the time, a mere 'sleeping giant' was Robbie O'Donnell, later to be known as Robbie Williams.

Activities

1. Find other examples of people whose potential was overlooked and who later became highly successful in their field (research people such as Van Gogh, the Beatles etc.).

2. Research and contact former pupils of your own school who have gone on to be successful in their education or chosen profession. Invite them back into school to talk about their early memories and how they went on to be successful in their professional context.
3. Set up a webpage on your school website for past pupils to communicate with present pupils and give accounts of their successes in later life.
4. Invite these pupils to academic award or prize evenings to contribute and give talks to current pupils about their potential.
5. Make contact with well-known people appearing at your local theatre etc. and invite them in to talk about their professional success and early potential.
6. Interview any of the above for a school/class magazine.

Transfer and Generalisation

We all have the potential within us to be as gifted as Einstein or as talented as Mozart. Our brains are basically built the same and have an enormous innate capacity for memory, understanding and performing at high levels of ability. So what can we do to make a difference?

Brain Byte

Each one of us has vast amounts of potential. Our brains have many hard-wired functions; programmes built into our brains to help us respond to and perform certain things at certain times in our lives. In human beings 80% of the brain's cortex has *no* other purpose than new learning.

School Reunion

Some people think that if we believe that the future is fixed then there is not much we can do to change things.

Others believe that the future is there to be invented. The Sony corporation has planning meetings to discuss what kind of products it would like to see up to one thousand years in the future. It is said that someone thought up the idea for the mobile phone from the hand-held 'communicators' in *Star Trek* that are used to communicate between the planet surfaces and the ship.

On a much more personal level, we want you to feel that you have control over your future. We want you to be optimistic and ambitious.

What predictions for the future can you make for yourself? What would you like to do in the next five years? Ten years? Twenty years?

Activity

Imagine there is going to be a school reunion in the year 2022. Each person has to give a short speech saying what they have achieved since leaving school. You can make this as imaginative as you like!

Chapter Three
If You Always Do ...

Comfort Zones and Risk

We all live with what psychologists sometimes call 'comfort zones'. A comfort zone is a place or an activity we feel comfortable with. For some of us this means sticking with what we know and not doing anything differently. I have a relative who refuses to try foreign food while on holiday and will happily eat the same meal every day rather than 'risk' something he has never tried before and so be 'out of his comfort zone'.

For other people, being out of their comfort zones can mean terrible feelings of embarrassment and fear. Having to speak in public, having their hair cut differently, speaking to someone they don't know, trying something new, visiting a place they have never seen before or doing something 'daring' will put them far out of their comfort zones. They will do anything to get back to their comfort zones where they feel safe.

Personal change and growth will never take place unless you occasionally step out of your comfort zone. Unless you try something different and allow your mind to grow there is a danger that you will be stuck in time and never change.

> If you always do what you've always done –
> you'll always get what you've always got.

Doing it differently might just be the key to solving the problem no one else has managed to crack. The scientist Stephen Hawking, who is paralysed through motor-neurone disease, has managed to make all sorts of amazing discoveries in physics because he has to think in symbols and pictures instead of writing things down. It is because he cannot write things down that his thought processes have had to be 'unusual' and therefore different from those of other scientists who have become stuck with the same problems.

A wise person once said, "Show me someone who never made a mistake and I'll show you someone who never made anything at all." Taking a risk that you might 'fail' could actually be the key to your success.

Jack and the Storytelling Contest

Now read this story about a person whose life is frozen in time because of his inability to take risks.

Every year the village held a storytelling contest at the inn on the edge of the lake. And everyone would gather to drink strong beer and eat the delicious food and listen to marvellous storytellers who came from all over the county to thrill the audience with their tales of magic and mystery and all sorts of wonderful deeds.

The villagers would fill their plates and gather wide-eyed around the large fire and listen to them compete for the two main trophies and prizes which were:

A large bottle of whiskey for the best story and a large bottle of brandy for the biggest lie.

It was a tradition of the evening for the compère to ask an unprepared member of the audience to stand and tell a story, but if they refused they were ordered to pay a forfeit, which usually consisted of some humiliating and menial task. Either that or pay a fine and be asked to leave the room.

Jack, a shy and lonely bachelor who worked on his father's isolated farm would creep in to the back of the room each year hoping not to be noticed, and secretly wish that he too could be like them and become a great storyteller. But sadly he knew that this was never likely to be, for he was too shy and led a lonely and uneventful life.

One year when he arrived at the contest a little later than usual, the compère saw him trying to sneak in and asked in a loud voice,

"You there, at the back."

"Who me?" answered Jack, his heart beating like a frog.

"Yes, it's Jack, isn't it? Come on lad, stand up and give us a story."

"Oh er, goodness me," mumbled Jack 'I don't know any!' and he suddenly felt very foolish as all eyes turned to him.

"Then you must pay a forfeit, my lad," answered the compère. "Mmm, what shall it be? Right, Jack, on the edge of the lake you will find a fishing boat which has been pulled up on the shore. Take this copper scoop and empty it of any water. And don't come back until it's completely dry."

When Jack closed the inn door and stepped out into the frosty, moonlit air he heard the loud laughter of the folk inside drift out with the smells of delicious foods as he made his way down to the water's edge with the copper scoop he had been given to complete the task.

"Bother!" he said "I shall always be lonely. Who'll ever be interested in me?"

He climbed into the boat and as he reached into his red waistcoat pocket for his small clay pipe the boat was suddenly pulled as if by an unseen force into the centre of the lake, flinging him back and knocking him unconscious.

Several hours must have passed because when he woke it was daylight and he assumed he had drifted a long way because none of the familiar sights on the shore were there for him to see.

In fact, things around him looked very strange indeed. It was while he was looking around that he happened to glance at his hands and instead of the red, callused hands of a labourer, he saw the pale, delicate hands of a young woman.

And when Jack looked down at his feet, instead of the heavy working boots he had worn previously there were pretty feminine shoes covering his very feminine feet.

Glancing over the edge of the boat, Jack examined his reflection in the lake. He saw now that he had been completely transformed in his appearance and clothing into a woman. Naturally he was confused and, as he stepped out of the boat, he began to sob in bewilderment and held his head in his hands.

"Can I help you?" said a voice suddenly.

Jack looked up to see a handsome young man gazing with obvious concern back at him. Not wishing to appear foolish, Jack muttered something about being lost, having banged his head and memory loss.

The young man invited Jack back to his mother's cottage at the edge of the lake where he was greeted with great hospitality. In fact the young man seemed very interested in Jack and over the next few days they became firm friends.

As Jack began to get used to his transformation he decided that perhaps things weren't all that bad after all, he was, in fact, quite attractive and now had lots of friends. The young man's mother cared for Jack as if he were her own daughter and it wasn't long before the young man was proposing marriage.

His previous life as a farm labourer now seemed little more than a dim memory and Jack settled into married life quite happily. After a year, the couple had a son and a year later a daughter and Jack was as content as he could have wished to be.

One evening, several years later, Jack was walking alone by the edge of the lake when over in the reeds he caught sight of something which seemed strangely familiar, and he walked down to take a closer look. It was the boat and on its bottom he saw a small clay pipe next to a bright copper scoop. As he bent to pick it up, the boat was suddenly pulled, as if by an unseen hand, towards the centre of the lake and Jack was flung back and knocked unconscious by its force.

When he awoke it was dark and the stars twinkled like frost in the sky. He looked down at his hands, his feet, his body – gone were the pretty clothes, the shoes, the pale, delicate skin and instead he saw the coarse red of a labourer's hands, the grimy work overalls of a farmer's son.

Quickly he leapt from the boat and ran up to the inn on the side on the lake where the storytelling contest was still in play. As he burst open the door the voices were suddenly silent as he shouted.

"Where's my husband? Where are my children?"

"Hold on a minute, Jack," said the compère, struggling not to smile, "Calm down a bit now, son. Have a glass of this strong beer and tell us all what's troubling you."

When Jack had finished telling his story, the compère raised his eyebrows and shook his head.

"Well, son," he said, pausing for effect, "That was not only the best story we have heard this evening, it has got to be the biggest lie."

And although Jack took home the bottle of whiskey, the bottle of brandy and the two coveted trophies that night, I'm not sure he went home a happy man.

(Garry Burnett *based on a traditional tale*)

I'm not sure that the ending of this story is a happy one, but the message in the story is quite powerful.

Questions

1. How did Jack's fear of stepping out of his comfort zone affect the things he did?
2. What was Jack initially afraid of?
3. How did this change through the story?
4. Can you make any connection between this extract and the 'Remarkable Story of Cliff Young'?

Transfer and generalisation

In 'Learning to Learn' we want you to recognise that to grow sometimes means taking a risk, doing something differently. This doesn't mean suddenly transforming and becoming the complete opposite of what you are now.

You might start by each day speaking to someone to whom you have never spoken before; by trying something from the menu of a restaurant or take-away that you would not normally have tried; by looking in a different shop from those you normally go to; by trying your hair in a different style; by arranging your bedroom differently; by buying or borrowing CDs you might not normally have listened to.

See yourself as someone who is prepared to take risks. Be like Cliff Young, who was mocked at first for being so different from all of the other athletes and then went on not only to win the race but to set the standard for how it should be run from then on.

'Failure', after all, is only a setback to you achieving your dreams.

Comfort Zones and Fear

> "It is in the night, imagining some fear
> How easy is a bush supposed a bear"
> (William Shakespeare – 'A Midsummer Night's Dream')

In the winter time, whenever my parents ask me to run an errand to Mrs Butter's corner shop at the end of our street, although I would never admit it, it always caused a great fluttering of panic to seize my chest. Our street was lined with an avenue of tall trees whose branches caused dark shadows to be cast over the pavement and the road, and the only light came from a string of dim street lamps, set wide apart and alternately on opposite sides of the road, or occasionally from the lighted windows of houses whose front curtains remained open.

Anybody who saw me step out onto the street, look around to see if there was anybody who I could walk near to, or any cars which would light up the street temporarily with their headlamps, would probably think they were watching a lunatic when they saw what happened next. You see, I was so afraid of the dark, that in my mind every darkened alcove contained bears, wolves or devils with hooked claws and wings, or some horror-film fiend, stalking me. So what I used to do was run from street lamp to street lamp, across the road and back until I reached the end of the street, about ten times the real distance because of the zig-zag route I had taken. If anyone I knew saw me and asked me what I was doing I would tell them I was 'in training', because I never dared admit the truth.

Going to Taylor's newsagents was even scarier because it then meant I had to run past the Sacred Heart Catholic church and a cowled statue of Mary next to a life-sized crucified Jesus (sometimes they haunted my dreams), and I would imagine that for a moment they would come alive, blink their eyes and turn towards me from the darkness.

Darkness … where I would make shapes and figures out of shadows that in the daytime simply didn't exist.

But then my dad and my Uncle Kevin didn't do anything to help. I sometimes think there was a kind of conspiracy between them to see who could frighten us the most. On Friday nights, my brother and me would be allowed to stay up late to watch the Hammer House of Horror, which often featured Count Dracula, the Werewolf, or the fiend who used to frighten me the most, 'Frankenstein's monster'. There were loads of Frankenstein films, 'The Bride of Frankenstein', 'The Curse of Frankenstein', 'Frankenstein meets Godzilla', and I wouldn't be surprised if there had been a 'Frankenstein meets Uncle Kevin' made somewhere, too horrific for general release.

I don't know what it was about the Frankenstein films in particular that used to scare me so much but when this expressionless, white-faced monster came lumbering out of the fog and you could see the horrific scars all over his hands and neck, I used to get ever so frightened. In one of them, he was holding the hand of this sweet little girl with ringlets, who had no idea that he was a psychopathic monster before he committed a terrible murder and a great crowd of angry, torch-bearing villagers would storm the castle, only to have boulders or boiling oil rained down upon them by Igor, the hunchback, cackling madly and with his hair blowing wildly. Believe me, I've had more than one screaming nightmare about running away while he chased me and slipping desperately on muddy ground, unable to escape.

But the worst thing about all of this was that my dad, who used to sit up to watch these films with us, used to pretend to fall asleep on the settee during the middle of them and then, when the music began building to a really scary bit and you just knew that something terrible was going to happen, he would suddenly sit bolt upright, shout and slap the arm of the settee.

And of course all of this made going to bed even harder because I shared a bedroom with my brother and we had this unwritten rule 'last one in bed turns the lights off'. It often led to fights, or one of us pushing the other one down the stairs, especially on nights when the Hammer House of Horror had been on, when we were even more scared at the prospect of running the six or seven feet from the light switch to the bed. Do you know, one night my brother even took a broom handle with him so he could switch off the light by poking it while he was lying in bed?

And then the room went dark and the night noises began.

In the summer time, when 'Billy Smart's Circus' pitched in the park near to where I lived, I would lie very still, listening to the trumpeting of elephants and roaring of lions, squeezing my eyes shut in the darkness in case a pair or green-spangled eyes blinked open from the dark corners of my bedroom and a huge beast behind them sat on its haunches, preparing to spring.

I soothed myself in situations like these by painting the scene a different colour, turning the dark colours of night into the bright ones of day, or by switching the light on in my mind and then getting up and actually walking around, telling myself how ridiculous I had been. Sometimes I would play my favourite tunes in my head or imagine the voice of someone I knew, talking to me and telling me not to worry. It was an action which took me out of my comfort-zone and made me confront what I was frightened of directly, but it was the only way I could relax and make the fear evaporate.

And even now, after all these years, and in situations where I am nervous or can't see my way ahead because of the darkness around me, I close my eyes and see myself, a boy still running, appearing and disappearing in occasional pools of light before I quickly turn on the bright colours of day.

(Taken from the short story 'A Star' by Garry Burnett)

Questions/Activity

Sometimes people don't take risks or do things because of unnecessary fear.

One of Tiger Woods's affirmations (see Chapter Six) is "I smile at obstacles". In other words, he changes the way he reacts, not the situation itself.

1. What was the young boy afraid of?
2. What do you think the boy in the story was *really* afraid of?
3. How did he deal with this fear as a young boy?
4. How did this change?
5. How do you cope with situations when you are frightened?
6. What do you do to help take on your fears?
7. How can you help yourself change the way you think about fear?

Write a similar story about something which has frightened you.

Chapter Four
Think You Can

"Whether you think you can or you think you can't, you're right"
(Henry Ford)

At the beginning of this extract from the screenplay of *The Empire Strikes Back*, Luke Skywalker is finding his training as a Jedi knight very difficult. Master Yoda is trying, without much success so far, to release the powers of 'the Force' within him. When he releases the positive energy of 'the Force' Luke will be able to accomplish almost anything he chooses, but first he needs to believe in himself.

Luke Trains to be a Jedi

Luke's face is upside-down and showing enormous strain. He stands on his hands, with Yoda perched on his feet. Opposite Luke and Yoda are two rocks the size of bowling balls. Luke stares at the rocks and concentrates. One of the rocks lifts from the ground and floats up to rest on the other.

YODA: Use the Force. Yes …

Yoda taps Luke's leg. Quickly, Luke lifts one hand from the ground. His body wavers, but he maintains his balance. Artoo, standing nearby, is whistling and beeping frantically.

YODA: Now … the stone. Feel it.

Luke concentrates on trying to lift the top rock. It rises a few feet, shaking under the strain. But, distracted by Artoo's frantic beeping, Luke loses his balance and finally collapses. Yoda jumps clear.

YODA: Concentrate!

Annoyed at the disturbance, Luke looks over at Artoo, who is rocking urgently back and forth in front of him. Artoo waddles closer to Luke, chirping wildly, then scoots over to the edge of the swamp. Catching on, Luke rushes to the water's edge. The X-wing fighter has sunk, and only the tip of its nose shows above the lake's surface.

LUKE: Oh, no. We'll never get it out now.

Yoda stamps his foot in irritation.

YODA: So certain are you. Always with you it cannot be done. Hear you nothing that I say?

Luke looks uncertainly out at the ship.

LUKE: Master, moving stones around is one thing. This is totally different.

YODA: No! No different! Only different in your mind. You must unlearn what you have learned.

LUKE: *(focusing, quietly)* All right, I'll give it a try.

YODA: No! Try not. Do. Or do not. There is no try.

Luke closes his eyes and concentrates on thinking the ship out. Slowly, the X-wing's nose begins to rise above the water. It hovers for a moment and then slides back, disappearing once again.

LUKE: *(panting heavily)* I can't. It's too big.

YODA: Size matters not. Look at me. Judge me by my size, do you? Hm? Mmmm.

Luke shakes his head.

YODA: And well you should not. For my ally is the Force. And a powerful ally it is. Life creates it, makes it grow. Its energy surrounds us and binds us. Luminous beings are we … *(Yoda pinches Luke's shoulder)* … not this crude matter *(a sweeping gesture)*. You must feel the Force around you *(gesturing)*. Here, between you … me … the tree … the rock … everywhere! Yes, even between this land and that ship!

LUKE: *(discouraged)* You want the impossible.

Quietly Yoda turns toward the X-wing fighter. With his eyes closed and his head bowed, he raises his arm and points at the ship. Soon, the fighter rises above the water and moves forward as Artoo beeps in terror and scoots away. The entire X-wing moves majestically, surely, toward the shore. Yoda stands on a tree root and guides the fighter carefully down toward the beach. Luke stares in astonishment as the fighter settles down onto the shore. He walks toward Yoda.

LUKE: I don't … I don't believe it.

YODA: That is why you fail.

(George Lucas, from *Star Wars: The Empire Strikes Back*)

Questions

1. Why does Luke fail?
2. What do you think Yoda means when he says "No! Try not. Do. Or do not. There is no try"?
3. How do you relate this extract to 'Learning to Learn'? What is the connection?

If …

If you think you are beaten you are
If you think you dare not, you don't
If you like to win, but think you can't
It's almost certain you won't.
If you think you'll lose you've lost
For out of the world we find
Success begins with a fellow's will
It's all in the state of mind.
If you think you're outclassed, you are
You've got to think high to rise
You've got to be sure of yourself before
You can ever win a prize.
Life's battles don't always go
To the stronger or faster man
But sooner or later the man who wins
Is the one who thinks he **can**.

(Anon.)

Activities

1. Write down what the *inspirational message* in the poem means to you.
2. How does it link with all of the information you have learnt about *self-esteem* so far?
3. Write a poem with a similar *inspiring* message.

29

Slogans for Success

Tenacity means having the courage to see your dreams through. Even when you think that all is lost you should never lose sight of your dreams and never give up. The feelings expressed in the lyrics to 'The Impossible Dream' (reprinted in Chapter Seven) and the words to Maya Angelou's poem 'Still I rise' (reprinted in Chapter Nine) illustrate this well.

"Keep your eyes on the prize" would be a good slogan or motto to keep in your head to sum up these feelings, or possibly this line from a Chumbawumba song: "I get knocked down, but I get up again. You ain't ever gonna keep me down".

Activities

1. Read the following slogans and mottoes. Choose one that you would like for yourself, or write one of your own.
   - Success comes in cans not can'ts
   - Whether you think you can or you think you can't, you're right
   - Your most valuable asset in life is a positive attitude
   - The only failure in life is the failure to try
   - If you're not asking questions, you're probably not learning
   - If you believe in yourself, you can and will succeed
   - A goal shared with someone else is a more powerful motivator than one you keep to yourself
   - The dictionary is the only place where effort comes after achievement
   - If at first you don't succeed – try, try and try again, but only after you have thought about it
2. Write an explanation of why the one that you have chosen or written would be a suitable slogan for success for you in particular.
3. Design a T-shirt with your own slogan for success on it.
4. Design an inspirational poster for your room with your own slogan for success on it.

My Inspirational T-shirt!

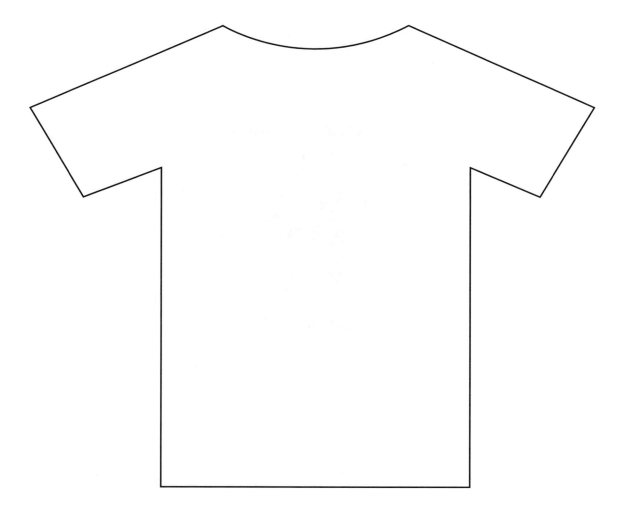

Chapter Five
Mission Impossible?

The Story of the Four-Minute Mile

Believe in yourself, even if no one else does.

The Story of the Four-Minute Mile

Believe in yourself, even if no one else does.

The story of how the four-minute mile was broken is a remarkable one. People had been attempting to achieve it since the days of the ancient Greeks. In fact folklore has it that the Greeks used lions to chase the runners in order to make them run faster. They also tried feeding them tiger's milk – not the stuff you get down at the health-food stores, but the real thing. Nothing worked. So they decided it was impossible. And for thousands of years everyone believed it: it was physiologically impossible for a human being to run a mile in under four minutes; our bone structure was all wrong; wind resistance too great; lung-power inadequate. There were a million reasons.

Then one man, one single human being, proved that the doctors, the trainers, the athletes, and the *millions and millions* before him who tried and failed, were all wrong. And, miracle of miracles, the year after Roger Bannister broke the four-minute mile, thirty-seven other runners broke the four-minute mile, and the year after that, three hundred runners broke the four-minute mile.

Today, you can watch a race where all the runners finish in under four minutes. In other words, the runner who finished last would have been regarded as having accomplished the impossible a few decades ago.

What happened? There were no great breakthroughs in training. Human bone structure did not suddenly improve. But human attitudes did!

Activities

1. Imagine you are Roger Bannister and you are being interviewed just after breaking the record. Write a short statement for the press giving your reactions to the news that you have broken the record.

2. What other achievements could human beings make if their attitudes changed? Make a list of things people might do in the future that are considered impossible now. (You might think about topics such as sport, travel, science etc.) Say why you think these things might be achieved in the future.

3. Write a list of things that you consider to be impossible for *you* to achieve. Say what the barriers are that stop you from achieving each of them.

'It Couldn't be Done'

Somebody said that it couldn't be done,
But she with a chuckle replied,
That maybe it couldn't, but she would be one
Who wouldn't say so till she tried.
So she buckled right in with the trace of a grin
On her face; if worried she hid it.
She started to sing as she tackled the thing
That couldn't be done and she did it.

Somebody scoffed: "Oh you'll never do that,
At least no one ever has done it."
And she took off her coat and she took off her hat,
And the first thing we knew she's begun it.
With a lift of her chin and a bit of a grin,
Without any doubting or quiddit,
She started to sing as she tackled the thing
That couldn't be done and she did it.

There are thousands to tell you it cannot be done,
There are thousands to prophesy failure,
There are thousands to point out to you, one by one,
The dangers that are sure to assail you.
But just buckle in with a bit of a grin,
Then take off your coat and go to it.
Just start in to sing as you tackle the thing
That cannot be done and *you'll do it*.

(Anon.)

Join the Dots

Join all the nine together with four straight lines. You must not take your pen or pencil off the paper. You have three attempts. No going over the same line twice!

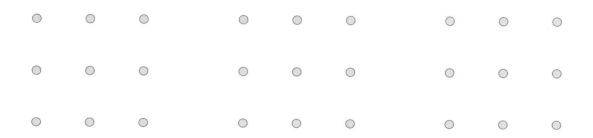

Join all the nine together with three straight lines. You must not take your pen or pencil off the paper. You have three attempts.

Join all the nine together with one straight line. You must not take your pen or pencil off the paper. You have three attempts.

What do you think you have learnt from this exercise?

Solution: See www.garryburnett.com

The Remarkable Story of Cliff Young

Cliff Young shocked the world of ultramarathon running in 1983 when he won Australia's big-time Sydney-to-Melbourne Race as a 61-year-old farmer. He covered the 875-kilometre distance in 5 days, 15 hours and 4 minutes, defeating legends like George Perdon, Siggy Bauer, John Hughes, Tony Rafferty and Bob Bruner. He is still running today.

The following article describes Cliff's sensational victory and a moral we can all draw from it.

In many ways, we do not act according to the *truth*. We act according to the truth as we *believe* it to be. Our beliefs cause us to act in a way that will lead to us succeeding or failing, regardless of how good we are, or well-rehearsed, or expert at the task. Nothing proves this better than the true story of Cliff Young.

In Australia the 875-km ultramarathon is held between the cities of Sydney and Melbourne. In 1983 a 61-year-old man named Cliff Young showed up to run the race. Now the world-class runners thought he was some practical joker who had showed up in the wrong place because Cliff showed up wearing overalls and galoshes. And he was obviously an old man.

The press were very interested in him and assumed that he was perhaps a fun-runner, not likely to last a day against the 'Nike'-sponsored big name professionals. When he told them he was there for the marathon, the professional runners asked if he had ever run in a marathon before. "No," replied Cliff. "How have you been training?" they asked. "I have cattle on my station [farm] and since I have no horses, I run around to move them along." The legend is that he started chasing his cows after his dog died. He barked like the dog so the cows would respond, thus building his lung power. While the others were eating and drinking power food, Cliff was eating potatoes.The runners and the whole watching world, it seemed, laughed.

You see, every professional marathoner *knew* with certainty that it took about 6 days to run this race, and that in order to compete, you would need to run 18 hours and sleep 6 hours. Cliff Young was clearly not up to their standards.

When the marathon started, the pros left Cliff behind in his galoshes. He had a leisurely shuffling style of running that targeted him as an amateur.

Cliff had no training. He did not *know* what the world-class runners *knew*. As you have probably guessed, Cliff won the race, but that is not what is astonishing. What is astonishing is that *he cut one and a half days off the record time*.

How? Because of his lack of training, he didn't 'know' that you had to sleep. Cliff just kept on shuffling along in his galoshes while the pro runners slept, and he finished the race in 5 days, 15 hours and 4 minutes. He beat everybody. He was a sensation in Australia.

Now that world-class runners 'know' that it is possible to run days at a time without sleep, and that they can conserve energy by adopting an easy shuffling jog, they have a new way of approaching long marathons.

We are like the pro runners. We act, not according to the 'real truth' but according to some truth given to us by some well-meaning or not-so-well-meaning 'expert'. For this reason, people that don't know the 'accepted wisdom', people who do or think differently, people who don't put 'barriers' in front of themselves, are more likely to discover new aspects of life, create remarkable inventions, and break through into a new realm of consciousness.

In his autobiography *Cliffy's Book* he gives an account of the final stages of the race:

"I started to get a woozy head. I was being smothered as we went along Sydney Road, through Coburg and on to Brunswick. I was choking. I needed clean air. After all I'd been through I didn't want it all to end for lack of clean air when I was so near.

"For seven hours, I'd gone non-stop, save for trips to the loo. No food, no drink, no sleep. I just wanted it to end. The momentum of all those people just kept pushing me along; I was caught in a wave pressing me towards a shore. Hell, George Perdon was then running second, but was 50 miles back. I could have crawled on all fours and still won …

"'Just a few more yards,' I said to myself through all the noise of fire engine sirens, fireworks and cheers from the crowd. The noise was deafening, and after marking practically every tree from Sydney to Melbourne, I was desperate to go to the loo again. I breasted the tape, my trip to hell and back over."

(Cliff Young, from *Cliffy's Book*)

Activity

1. Imagine you are a news reporter. Make a list of questions you would like to ask Cliff Young.
2. Interview other runners from the race, giving their reactions to his great victory.
3. Design the front page of a newspaper for the day after Cliff Young's historic run.

Chapter Six
Affirmations

Turning Goals into Affirmations

Read the following extract about the childhood of the great golfer Tiger Woods.

Tiger Woods – Born to Reign

Tiger was a kid, but not in the traditional sense. When he was still only six, he listened to tape recordings with subliminal (hidden) messages to help him develop a stronger sense of self-control and discipline. Earl (his father) had seen them in a store and bought them for his son, carefully explaining why he should listen to them. The boy understood. He played them on a cassette player in his room, hearing only the flow of water down a creek, or soft music, but the messages began to imbue themselves in his sub-conscious:

> *I will my own destiny.*
> *I believe in me.*
> *I smile at obstacles.*
> *I am firm in my resolve.*
> *I fulfil my resolutions powerfully.*
> *My strength is great.*
> *I stick to it, easily, naturally.*
> *My will moves mountains.*
> *I focus and give it my all.*
> *My decisions are strong.*
> *I do it with all my heart.*

The messages were inscribed on paper as well, and he tacked them to the walls of his room, as reinforcement. He listened to the tapes so often he wore them out. He began to apply them instantly. He was still only six when he went to the Optimist Junior World 'ten and under' division at Presidio Hills in San Diego, his first international tournament. At the first tee, his father reassured him that whether he won or lost was not the point – either way he should have fun. Tiger then ripped his shot down the middle.

Later, Earl asked Tiger what he was thinking about as he stood over the ball on the first tee. "Where I wanted the ball to go, Daddy," he said, shocking his unsuspecting father, who wasn't sure the subliminal messages would take hold so quickly. The negative thoughts that typically invade the minds of young, uncertain athletes were not there. Tiger was nervous – even today he acknowledges an uneasy stomach at the first tee – but he suppressed his nervousness by visualising the shot, an instrumental part of a professional golfer's preshot routine.

(John Strege, from *Tiger: A Biography of Tiger Woods*)

Discuss

What was it about Tiger's approach to life that contributed towards making him successful?

Affirmations of Success

A recent study was published of the top 2% of high achievers who are acknowledged to be at the top of their particular field (the study covered a wide range of fields, including sport, business and the arts). While the subjects undoubtedly had very high self-esteem, more notable was the fact that from a very early age they were all 'single-minded' about achieving their goals in life – and, particularly, were determined that nothing would get in their way.

While they all enjoyed different kinds of success, they all, however, had one thing in common. They had *written down* their goals in life.

Once you have a clear idea of what you want to do or be in life, you should try to write these goals down in the form of an *affirmation*. This is a very powerful form of thinking that encourages you to work towards how you see yourself in the future. Read again Tiger Woods's affirmations:

> I will my own destiny.
> I believe in me.
> I smile at obstacles.
> I am firm in my resolve.
> I fulfil my resolutions powerfully.
> My strength is great.
> I stick to it, easily, naturally.
> My will moves mountains.
> I focus and give it my all.
> My decisions are strong.
> I do it with all my heart.

They gave him the mental strength and concentration to make his goals become reality. But notice how these are written. Not once does Tiger ever say "I would like to …" or "I want to …" – he writes down his aims as *affirmations*:

- as if they had already happened;
- as if they were already true;
- as if he had already achieved them.

Wannabes and Affirmations

If we say we 'want' to do something then we've said something that is already true. We already want to do it. To create motivation and energy in our minds we need to see ourselves doing something that is not already true. Think of the times when you have been feeling hungry and you can almost taste the delicious meal being cooked, or think of the time when you just had to buy that new skirt or pair of jeans that you can just 'see yourself' looking great in.

The effect on our mind and our *motivation* can be very powerful when we write down our goals in the form of affirmations. We start to see the 'new' us and work very quickly and determinedly to resolve the picture – to make it happen. This idea comes from a school of thought called 'Gestalt' psychology.

Most New Year's resolutions fail in the first week of January because they are 'wannabes' – I want to be a better footballer; I want to do my homework on time; I want to keep my room tidy. In order to feel 'Gestalt', try imagining this situation: you are at home and your mum or dad phones you to say, "Did you do the dishes and make your bed as you promised?" Even though you have not, you say, "Yes." Just to add further proof to your mum that you are a wonderful son or daughter, you say that not only have you done the dishes and made your bed, you also made the tea, hoovered the carpets and polished the table.

Now you've done it! Suddenly, through the mismatch or 'Gestalt' we feel very uneasy and find it hard to relax because the situation before us does not match the one we have described to our parent on the phone. So, quickly we move to do the things we said and to make the picture we described come into reality.

Many times I have heard people tell me, as a teacher, something like the following: "Oh yes, Mr Burnett, I've done my homework. I did three pages and I word-processed it neatly and answered every question. I just left it on the table at home." Only later have they confessed that they had not even started it when they said this. Strangely, the act of describing it as *if* it were already done gave them the extra energy to complete it.

How can we use this powerful technique to make ourselves more ambitious, more confident and better motivated as learners?

Easy! We should write down our great dreams and goals for our lives as affirmations.

Writing Affirmations

There are three important ingredients in an 'affirmation':

It should always be written in the   *first person*
It should always be written in the   *present tense*
It should always be a   *positive achievement*

For example
You might have a goal or target you wish to achieve and it might be:

"I want always to do my homework on time."

41

1. Check that it is in the *first person* (this one is):
2. Change it to the *present tense*:

    I *always do* my homework on time.

3. Add some positive emotion:

    I feel very *proud* and *relaxed* that ...

And so you have your affirmation:

> *"I feel very proud and relaxed that I always do my homework on time."*

Writing Affirmations – Another Short Cut

Problem

Stage 1
Imagine you have a problem:

> *"I never seem to get my homework done on time."*

Stage 2
How do you feel as a result?

> *"I feel nervous and unhappy about going into the next lesson when I might be told off or get into trouble."*

Solution

Stage 1
What would it be like if you did not have the problem?

> *"I always get my homework done before the deadline ..."*

Stage 2

How do you feel as a result?

> *"... and I feel very proud, relaxed and happy to go to the next lesson ready to learn."*

Affirmation

> *"I always get my homework done before the deadline and I feel very proud, relaxed and happy to go to the next lesson ready to learn."*

How to Make the Affirmation SMART

If, for example, I made the affirmation "I am happy and proud to be the top scorer in the netball team", I would be very foolish to think that this would be enough to make it happen without my having to do anything else. So I would need then to set goals and targets that will help me achieve the affirmation or become what I am affirming.

Supposing I were to affirm "I am a confident speller and hardly ever make a mistake in my work", I would then need to find a way to make this happen.

Do not worry about the way to make it happen *before* you make the affirmation, otherwise you will never get started.

You should now think about short steps or goals on the way to making *your* affirmation come true. These will need to be **SMART** targets:

Specific	means be particular – do not waffle or be general;
Measurable	put numbers or quantities on your affirmation (say how much);
Attainable	be **R**ealistic – "I want to run a sub-four-minute mile before I am 13" is probably a bit ambitious;
Timebound	give yourself dates and times to complete by.

Suppose you were to make the following affirmation:

"I am a confident speller and hardly ever make a mistake in my work."

Now you should apply the SMART targets:

Specific	*Which* words do I wish to learn to spell accurately (*ten a week*)?
Measurable	*How many (150 key words)?*
Attainable	*Can I* achieve this?
Realistic	Am I setting my sights *too high*?
Timebound	*When by (Half-term)?*

When you have written out your affirmations, practise writing some SMART targets to go with them.

If the affirmation is a strong picture in your mind you will begin to search for ways to complete the picture – to make the affirmation come true.

Chapter Seven
Food for Thought

Musical Affirmations

'The Greatest Love of All', recorded by George Benson, is thought by many people to have 'inspirational lyrics', which means it helps people to think positively about how they might want to live or change their lives.

Chumbawumba wrote a song with the chorus "I get knocked down, but I get up again …". You could apply that slogan to your life – always picking yourself up to carry on, even when you have setbacks.

Try to find other examples of songs with 'inspirational messages'. See the examples 'Moonshadow' by Cat Stevens, 'Something Inside So Strong' by Labi Siffre (both included here), 'I Will Survive', 'The Impossible Dream' or 'My Way'.

Of course most countries have national anthems, which are often sung on patriotic occasions like major sporting events, and their function is to lift people's spirits and make them feel aroused to support their country.

In the television series *Ally McBeal* the main characters have songs that they use as personal anthems. In the case of John Cage it is usually a Barry White song, which makes him feel macho and sexy. They play the songs in their heads to lift their spirits and make themselves feel more confident. In other words, they draw inspiration from the lyrics.

Activities

1. What do you interpret as the inspirational message in the extracts from these three songs: 'The Greatest Love of all'; 'Moonshadow'; 'So Strong'? (Your teacher may play one or more of these to you.)
2. Choose a song whose lyrics have made you think or have inspired you in some way.
3. Copy out the lyrics of your inspirational song in your exercise book.
4. Try to sum up in a sentence what it is about your song that you find inspirational.
5. Write an extra verse to that song.
6. Write your own 'personal anthem'. Specify what tune it should be sung to.

Transfer

Try singing or humming the song just before you have to do something challenging. See if your mood and attitude towards completing the task can change.

Sometimes simply a tune (without lyrics) can have the same motivating effect: think of the theme music to *Gladiators* or the *Rocky* films or *Mission: Impossible*. Choose a tune that will be your 'success theme tune'. Imagine you can hear the tune in your head every time you are about to learn or do something challenging.

Taken from 'Moonshadow'

And if I ever lose my hands, lose my plough, lose my land,
Oh if I ever lose my hands, Oh if … I won't have to work no more.
And if I ever lose my eyes, if my colours all run dry,
Yes if I ever lose my eyes, Oh if … I won't have to cry no more.

And if I ever lose my legs, I won't moan, and I won't beg,
Yes if I ever lose my legs, Oh if … I won't have to walk no more.
And if I ever lose my mouth, all my teeth, north and south,
Yes if I ever lose my mouth, Oh if … I won't have to talk …

Oh, I'm bein' followed by a moonshadow, moonshadow, moonshadow
Leapin' and hoppin' on a moonshadow, moonshadow, moonshadow
Did it take long to find me? I asked the faithful light.
Did it take long to find me? And are you gonna stay the night?

Oh, I'm bein' followed by a moonshadow, moonshadow, moonshadow
Leapin' and hoppin' on a moonshadow, moonshadow, moonshadow

(Cat Stevens (Yusuf Islam))

Taken from '(Something Inside) So Strong'

The higher you build your barriers
The taller I become
The further you take my rights away
The faster I will run
You can deny me, you can decide
To turn your face away
No matter 'cause there's

Something inside so strong
I know that I can make it
Though you're doing me wrong, so wrong
You thought that my pride was gone, oh no
There's something inside so strong
Oh, something inside so strong

Brothers and sisters, when they insist we're just not good enough
Well we know better, just look him in his eyes and say
We're gonna do it anyway, we're gonna do it anyway

(Labi Siffre)

'The Greatest Love of All'

I believe that children are our future
Teach them well and let them lead the way
Show them all the beauty they possess inside
Give them a sense of pride
To make it easier
Let the children's laughter
Remind us how we used to be

Everybody's searching for a hero
People need someone to look up to
I never found anyone who fulfilled my need
A lonely place to be
So I learned to depend on *me*
I decided long ago
Never to walk in anyone's shadow
If I fail, if I succeed
At least I'll live as I believe
No matter what they take from me
They can't take away my dignity

Because the greatest love of all
Is happening to me
I found the greatest love of all
Inside of me

The greatest love of all
Is easy to achieve
Learning to love yourself
Is the greatest love of all

And if by chance you find the place
That you've been dreaming of
Leads you to a lonely place
Find your strength in love

Words by Linda Creed
Music by Michael Masser
©1977 EMI Gold Horizon Music Corp and EMI Worldwide print rights
controlled by Warner Bros. Publications Inc/IMP Ltd
Reproduced by permission of International Music Publications Ltd

The Impossible Dream

To dream the impossible dream
To fight the unbeatable foe
To bear with unbearable sorrow
To run where the brave dare not go

To right the unrightable wrong
To be better far than you are
To try when your arms are too weary
To reach the unreachable star

This is my quest, to follow that star
No matter how hopeless, no matter how far
To be willing to give when there's no more to give
To be willing to die so that honor and justice may live
And I know if I'll only be true to this glorious quest
That my heart will lie peaceful and calm when I'm laid to my rest

And the world will be better for this
That one man, scorned and covered with scars,
Still strove with his last ounce of courage
To reach the unreachable star

(Joe Darion, from 'Man Of La Mancha')

Questions

1. What do you think "To reach the unreachable star" means?
2. Explain the lyrics of this song to someone who is unfamiliar with them: in simple language, what does the narrator intend to do?
3. What kind of person do you think would make these affirmations?

Chapter Eight
Inspiration ...

Benchmarking Success

"Every blade of grass has its angel that bends over it and whispers, 'Grow, grow.'"
(Anon)

Activities

1. Have you ever met anybody famous? Who was it?
   (a) Share interesting stories of encounters with famous people with the whole class. What kind of celebrity were they?
   (b) Discuss with a partner or in a group the time you met a well-known person. Were they pleasant, 'different', grumpy? Were they as you expected them to be?
2. Write a paragraph starting, "The day I met ...".
3. Think of categories you could put celebrities into, for example 'sports star', 'pop star', 'chance star' (e.g. 'somebody who has just been in the news'). Try to fill in ten examples in each of your six categories using the table below.

Sports	Chance	Pop			
Lennox-Lewis		Robbie Williams			

4. Conduct a survey in the class to see who has met whom in the different 'celebrity' categories. Survey other year groups, teachers and parents. Using your categories, produce graphs to see which category of celebrity is the most 'accessible'.

5. In your opinion what are the special qualities of a celebrity? Can you make up a good definition of what the word means? Which kind of celebrity do you admire most? Why? Discuss these questions in a group or as a class.

Activities

Celebrity factfile

Make up a fact sheet entitled "Ten things you might not know about my hero/heroine".

   Be ready to give a short presentation to the class, saying why you admire the person you have chosen.

Photograph of celebrity

1. _____

    _____

2. _____

    _____

3. _____

    _____

4. _____

_____

5. _____

_____

6. _____

_____

7. _____

_____

8. _____

_____

9. _____

_____

10. _____

_____

Celebrity 10 questions

Imagine that you are a well-known person. In groups of four, play "Guess my name in ten", using only "yes" or "no" answers.

For example, if you chose to be Madonna the questions/answers might be:

1.	Is the person male?	No
2.	Is she American?	Yes
3.	Is she a sports star?	No
4.	Is she in the music business?	Yes
5.	Is she a solo artist?	Yes

(etc., until your identity has been guessed or ten questions have been asked.)

You might choose a bizarre category of celebrity like 'cartoon star' and be Lisa Simpson! (Nobody said you couldn't!)

An audience with …

In the film *Bill and Ted's Excellent Adventure*, Bill and Ted, two American high-school students, travel through time to meet famous historical figures who help them out with their history assignment. For example, they bring back Napoleon to help with their paper on the French Revolution.

Imagine you could travel through time to interview anyone you have admired from the past, *but* for 30 minutes only. You must prepare for your interview well. It could be the most important interview you will ever do.

Write down your reasons for wanting to meet this person and carefully prepare a list of questions you would like to ask him or her.

Celebrity letter

Write a letter to someone you admire (a celebrity, writer, musician, scientist, TV personality etc.) asking for any advice or encouragement the person can give to help you achieve your goals. Try to ask questions whose answers will help you understand how your addressee became good at what he or she does.

Forwarding addresses can be found on many 'celebrity address' sites on the Internet. For example, 'Celebrity Address Emporium' and 'The Celebrity Address' Book.

Some advice for writing your letter
1. Keep the letter brief.
2. Explain who you are and why you are writing.
3. Send only a letter (a favourite photograph of yourself will probably go in the bin!).
4. Write something original and interesting. Try not to ask obvious questions like "How did you get into acting/pop music/writing etc." – although these are very valid questions they have probably been asked a thousand times before.
5. Enclose a self-addressed envelope (with postage).
6. Be patient – remember some of these people work away from home quite a lot and do not have the chance to answer fan mail every day.

Sending your letter
Apart from the many websites which give contact addresses, television companies will often forward mail to people who appear on their programmes. The main BBC office address is:

BBC Television Centre
Wood Lane
LONDON
W12 7RJ

Other companies can easily be found using Internet searches.

A sample letter

Dear Miss Roberts,

I am a pupil at Bash Street School, Gotham City, East Yorkshire. *In our 'Learning to Learn' lessons we are studying successful people in order to try to find out how they became successful at what they do.* At the moment I am studying drama at drama class and I would like to be an actress when I leave school. I have appeared as Sandy in *Grease* and the third wise man in our school play and I wondered if you could help me by answering these questions.

In the film *Notting Hill* you play an actress who, at one point, has difficulty learning her lines. How do you learn your lines accurately?

When you were at school, did you ever appear in a school play?

Do you have a personal motto or slogan?

If there were to be a remake of any film and you were to be the star, what would you like that film to be and which part would you like to have?

I would be very grateful if you could find the time to reply.

Yours sincerely,

Joe King

Now send off your letter and wait for a reply!

Transfer and Generalisation

We can learn such a lot from the great people of the past. Try to read biographies of people who have been successful in your chosen field, watch videos of their life stories, research their backgrounds on the Internet. Most people who became good at doing something did so because they 'emulated' their idols or people who were better than them.

Look at the work of the more able older pupils who have covered the same topics as you and talk to people who have already sat an exam similar to the one you are about to take.

Benchmark the best and try to discover what it is that they did to make them the best.

Anchors Aweigh!

One very powerful technique for connecting positive feelings with the challenge ahead of you is a technique taken from Neuro-Linguistic Programming (NLP) called 'anchoring'.

States of mind are often represented by physical movements. For example:

- Deep thinking or concentration can be signified by 'touching the chin';
- Approval can be represented by a 'thumbs-up'.

We are going to learn to anchor positive states of mind with our own little ritual that is quite easy to learn and very effective to practise.

Step 1

I would like you to think of your favourite 'Magic Moment' (think back to Chapter One of this book). As you do so, *press together your thumb and index finger* quite firmly. Use all of your senses to relive the magic moment in your mind.

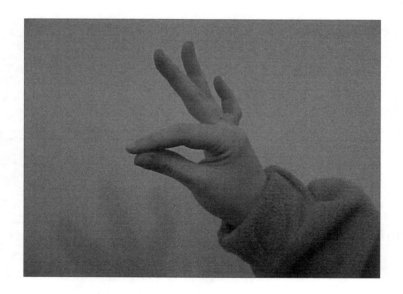

Step 2

Now think of the *person* you love the most, or the person who gives you the most encouragement or who is the most positive influence on your life. This might even be the person whom you admire the most and wish to 'benchmark'.

As you see this person's face and hear his or her voice (and even perhaps imagine the two of you are having a cuddle!), *press together your thumb and middle finger*.

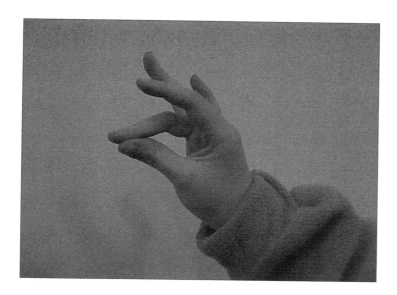

Step 3

Next think of a place where you have felt happy and safe – a place where you were able to relax and be contented. As you experience in your imagination the sights, sounds, smells and feelings you have in this place, *press together your thumb and ring finger* like this:

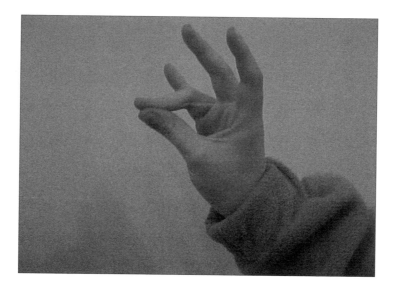

Quickly run through the routine, seeing in your mind's eye, as you press each finger against your thumb, a visualisation of the moment, person or place you chose.

Step 4

Now think of the challenge ahead. It could be that homework or assignment you have to do. Perhaps you are about to play a sports match or enter a competition. Whatever it is, as you *press your thumb and little finger together*, see yourself completing the task successfully, achieving your best in whatever you have chosen to do. Visualise yourself finishing the task positively, cheerfully and with pride.

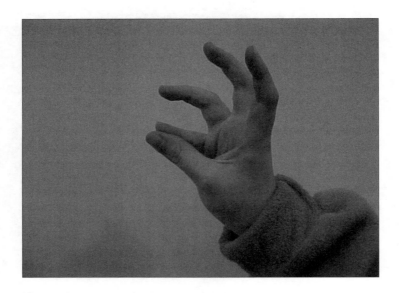

Once again run through the routine. Of course each of these anchors could change as time passes and as you achieve even better and greater things.

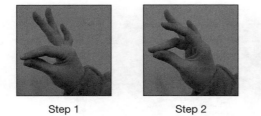 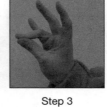 

| Step 1 | Step 2 | Step 3 | Step 4 |

Activity

Draw around your hand. On the fingers of this hand write your 'moment', 'person' and 'place'. Leave the little finger blank for writing your 'target' on.

Chapter Nine
Emotional Intelligence

'SERIOUS' Emotional Intelligence

What Does it Mean to be Intelligent?

In a recent book called *Emotional Intelligence*, Daniel Goleman claims that there is another very important way that people show that they are intelligent at 'solving problems', 'acting effectively' and 'making things'. He calls this 'EQ' (emotional quotient), as opposed to 'IQ' (intelligence quotient). Daniel Goleman suggests that the way people handle different kinds of emotional conflict in their lives is just as important as other kinds of 'academic' intelligence.

Goleman categorises Emotional Intelligence as follows:

- **Self-motivation**
- **Empathy**
- **Reflection**
- **Impulse control**
- **Optimism**
- **Understanding relationships**
- **Self-awareness**

This spells the word 'SERIOUS'.

Try to learn the list so that you can remember all seven of the categories. Some of these ideas you have explored already in earlier sections of 'Learning to Learn'. For example, 'Optimism' and 'Self-motivation' were introduced in all of the early work on self-esteem you did.

We will now explore some of these ideas in greater detail.

'Understanding Relationships' and 'Empathy'

"You never really understand a person until you climb inside their skin and walk around a little"
(Atticus Finch in Harper Lee, *To Kill a Mockingbird*)

We are going to begin thinking about emotional intelligence by looking at the story of Terry Dobson's encounter with a violent and drunken lout in Tokyo, adapted from Daniel Goleman's book *Emotional Intelligence*.

One of the most important skills of emotional intelligence is the ability to understand what motivates other people to do and say the things they do. Being able to 'get inside people's heads' and to be understanding about how they act and think is called 'empathy'.

The next step is to follow that with the ability to act effectively for the benefit of all concerned. This emotional skill will make us much more effective as learners in group work, for example, and in being able to cope better with the less considerate behaviour of others.

Terry Dobson and the Japanese Drunk

Read the following story with your teacher and then discuss some of the 'issues' or ideas it raises.

> If a test of emotional intelligence is the ability to understand and calm the sometimes distressing behaviour of others then handling someone at the peak of their rage has got to be the sign of mastery. Effective strategies for dealing with very angry and violent people might include 'empathising' with the person concerned and then distracting them from the feelings which have sent them out of control. Making them think in a more positive way.

> In the 1950s Terry Dobson was one of the first Westerners to study the martial art of Aikido in Japan. One afternoon he was riding home on a suburban train when a huge, very drunk and dirty labourer got on. The man, staggering, began

terrorising the passengers; screaming curses and even taking a swing at a woman holding a baby, sending her sprawling into the laps of an elderly couple, who then jumped to join the stampede to the other end. The drunk then grabbed the metal pole in the middle of the car with a roar and began to try to tear it out of its socket.

At that point, Terry, who was in peak physical condition from his daily eight-hour Aikido workouts, felt called on to intervene, in case someone should get seriously hurt. He recalled the words of his teacher: "Aikido is the art of reconciliation. Whoever has the mind to fight has broken his connection with the universe. If you try to dominate people you are already defeated. We study how to resolve conflict, not how to start it."

Indeed, Terry had agreed upon beginning his lessons never to pick a fight and to use his martial-arts skills only in defence. Now at last Terry saw a chance to test his Aikido abilities in real life, in what was clearly a legitimate opportunity. So while the other passengers sat frozen in their seats, Terry stood up slowly and with deliberation.

Seeing him the drunk roared, "Aha! A foreigner! You need a lesson in Japanese manners!" and began gathering himself to take on Terry.

But just as the drunk was on the verge of making his move, someone gave an ear-splitting oddly joyous shout: "Hey!"

The shout had the cheery note of someone who had suddenly come upon a fond friend. The drunk, surprised, spun around to see a tiny Japanese man, probably in his seventies, sitting there in a kimono. The old man beamed with delight at the drunk, and beckoned him over with a light wave of his hand and a lilting "C'mere."

The drunk strode over with a belligerent "Why the hell should I talk to you?"

Meanwhile Terry was ready to fell the drunk if he made the least violent move.

"What'cha been drinking?" the old man asked, his eyes beaming at the drunken labourer.

"I've been drinking sake, and it's none of your business," the drunk bellowed.

"Oh that's wonderful, absolutely wonderful," the old man replied in a warm tone. "You see, I love sake too. Every night, me and my wife (she's seventy-six you know) we warm up a bottle of sake and take it out into the garden, and we sit on an old wooden bench ..." He continued on about the persimmon tree in his backyard, the fortunes of his garden, enjoying sake in the evening.

The drunk's face began to soften as he listened to the old man: his fists unclenched. "Yeah ... I love persimmons too ..." his voice trailed off.

"Yes," the old man replied in a sprightly voice, "and I'm sure you have a wonderful wife."

"No," said the labourer. "My wife died ..." Sobbing, he launched into a sad tale of losing his wife, his home, his job, of being ashamed of himself.

Just then the train came to Terry's stop, and as he was getting off he turned to hear the old man invite the drunk to join him and tell him all about it, and to see the drunk sprawl along the seat, his head in the old man's lap.

That is emotional brilliance.

(Daniel Goleman, from *Emotional Intelligence*)

Reflection

1. What do you think the drunken man was hoping to achieve by his behaviour?
2. How did Terry initially want to solve the situation?
3. What did the old man do that Terry realised was much more effective?
4. What could this story teach us about coping with the tempers of others?

Discuss

1. How do we cope with our own tempers?
2. How good are we at understanding the feelings of others? (Often, I suspect, not as good as we would like to be.)

A Yuletide Tale

Activity

The following story is also available in the pack on audio CD. Listen to the story carefully and follow the words in your book. As you listen, be prepared to:

1. Discuss your favourite parts of the story.
2. Make a list of questions you would like to ask the author.
3. Attempt to 'visualise' scenes from the story – see them in your 'mind's eye'.
4. Reflect on the use of music to express emotion.

"The day will come when, after harnessing space, the winds, the tides and gravitation, we shall harness for God the energies of love. And on that day, for the second time in the history of the world, we shall have discovered fire"
(Pierre Teilhard de Chardin, French philosopher)

You could always tell the kids who'd got new bikes for Christmas because at about quarter to six on Christmas morning they'd be riding up and down the pavements outside our front window, heaving at their pedals, their bums sticking up in the air like jockeys' because their seats weren't quite adjusted to their size yet. Mind you, I was no different. I remember the Christmas I asked for a Raleigh Olympus 'racer'. It was the first big bike I'd ever had and it proved to me at last that I must be really 'grown-up'. All the others I'd had would seem like toys in comparison and for months before I used to day-dream about all of the places I'd be able to go on *my* new bike.

But then Christmas always began really early in our house and we always used to build up to it by saying things like:

"In two weeks and three days we'll be able to say 'It's Christmas this month'" or "Tomorrow will be the eve of the eve of the eve of the eve of Christmas Eve". That's what it was like in our house, we couldn't wait for Christmas.

I don't know how our parents managed to give us all they did when money was so tight. "The good old days?" Nana used to say. "They was bad. We had nowt. There were no credit cards or cheque books. We couldn't afford clothes for your Uncle Kevin until he was four, and then we bought him a vest so he could look out the window."

I think she was kidding about the last bit.

For about six months before Christmas we used to pay a shilling a week into a 'diddle 'em' at my mum's work. It was our pocket money and a good way, we thought, to save for presents. I always used to wonder why they called it a 'diddle 'em' until one year we didn't get any money because the woman who'd organised it had diddled everyone and spent it on bingo. But as soon as we did we would plan our Christmas shopping expedition 'on road'. It's funny going down Holderness Road for me even now because up to Craven Street not much has really changed. Even Aubrey's Discount SuperSave, the poor man's Fortnum and Mason's, where we used to buy most of our Christmas presents, is still there. But it contained everything that we needed and (and this was important) at 'affordable' prices. Bath cubes, bath salts, knitted bath salt jar covers that looked like French poodles, 'Pagan Beast After Shave' and all sorts of brassy ornaments and pictures of crying children that our aunties and uncles must have been *really grateful* for. The range of presents was endless and it was all 'under one roof'. Do you know one year from my brother I got a packet of Aubrey's SuperSave 'Christmas glitter' for a present!

"Oh thank you, it's just what I've always wanted," I lied.

I wouldn't have minded but he'd used half of it to brighten up the Christmas wrapping paper on the presents he'd bought.

"Oh no, I don't think he's been!" my dad teased as he shouted up the stairs on Christmas morning while we waited at the top, poised to practically fall down to get to our presents when he'd raked the ashes and lit the fire. "Oh, hold on, what's this? Come on then!" And then we tumbled down the stairs, fighting to get to the spot on the settee or chair where our pile of presents would be.

"Oh wow, look!" said my brother. "An *Adventure Kit*. Is the gun real, Dad?"

My sister had a doll that 'weed' and a beauty salon "for junior models and aspiring film stars", complete with real scissors for styling your doll's hair, hair curlers and make-up.

And there it was; six-speed, with gleaming chrome and clean tyres, my racer.

"Can I go out on it, Dad?"

"No, you can't. It's only a quarter past five and besides you've got no lights."

Do you remember the films that used to be shown at Christmas? It was different then, because there were no videos, and a new film at Christmas was a real event, a treat. After Leslie Crowther had visited the poorly children in the hospital and just before the Queen, on Christmas afternoon I remember one of my favourites being shown that year, *Lassie*. Lassie was this really clever dog that used to save people when they needed rescuing and she had all sorts of adventures. Actually, I think the film this particular Christmas was called *Lassie Comes Home* but it didn't matter because they all had practically the same heart-rending story and I would hide behind my comic when the sad violin music began to play, hoping that nobody, especially my dad or Uncle Kevin would see my eyes fill with tears at the inevitable bit when Lassie nearly died.

"Erhhmm, I'm going to play out on my bike now," I gulped.

"Aaaggh, look at him, he's crying!" Uncle Kevin shrieked.

"No. No, I'm not," I lied, hurrying outside so I could fiddle with my bike but at the same time sneaking a look through the back window to make sure Lassie was safe. But it was too late; they'd seen me cry now and they soon closed in for the kill, pointing and cackling.

"Get lost!" I shouted. "I'll run away."

"On your bike?" said Uncle Kevin. "Don't you mean you'll *ride* away?"

"They ought to call you 'Lassie'," said my dad, "… roaring at a film."

"Here," said Uncle Kevin. "Put one of your sister's dresses on and we'll sit you on the top of the Christmas tree!"

"Right that's it. I'm … going." I cried, and I slammed the door so hard I thought the glass would fall out.

"Come back, son," said my mum. "Take no notice of them. They'll only do it more."

"They don't care about me! Nobody cares so I'm going," and I wheeled my bike angrily to the ten-foot outside, scraping my leg on the pedal as I did. I lingered near the gate, looking around once or twice to see if they'd come for me and say sorry, but they didn't. And once or twice I even thought I saw them waving.

"I'll show them," I said to myself, tightening the grey, fur-rimmed hood of my khaki parka around my head. "I won't come back until really late, or maybe even tomorrow, and then they'll worry." I pushed uneasily at the pedals as I headed down Telford Street and on to Holderness Road. East Park gates were locked so I turned and headed right, past the cold, empty, closed-up shops and garages, out towards Holderness and the open country.

Though my eyes and nose were streaming and my hands were chapped red with cold, I didn't stop until I came to Thirtleby Lane, a narrow road between Sproatley and Coniston at a bend in the lane near a tumble-down barn. I leaned my bike against the hedge and kneeled on the damp grass.

And there I sat, all alone, on Christmas afternoon with the cold seeping through my black 'sannies', as my breath plumed out in front of me like grey ghosts. I looked back at the twinkling lights of the city, yellow and white against the winter sky as the afternoon began to pink into dust.

They didn't care that I was on my own. All they cared about was getting drunk and laughing at me.

For a while I just listened.

My pulse thumped gently in my temples from the exertion of the ride. Somewhere across the field crows "kaa-arked" from twiggy nests that clotted the tops of bare trees and a ragged robin busied in the autumn debris of the hedgerow.

Just then I thought I heard the faint calling of children as they played in the wood behind me, and it was as I stood up and turned, I saw him. A little boy standing alone at a gap in the wood, garlanded by trees. A small pale boy, lonely at the end of the hedgerow where the fields converged, and he was dressed in exactly the same clothes as me.

I rode quickly now, chased by the gathering darkness back to the light of the city and my home. Past mud-crusted farms and bungalow front rooms jumping with shadows of televisions and evening fires, until finally I turned into the ten-foot at the back of our house.

"Now where have *you* been?" said my mum, gently, as I leaned my bike against the wall. "I've been so worried about you. Come on." And she pressed my damp head against her waist.

I looked through the window at Uncle Kevin and my dad fast asleep on the settee. From where I stood in the darkness it reminded me of one of those crib scenes for the Nativity, though there was something strange about *them*, and what it was I just couldn't make out.

"I've got something to show you," she said, holding my hand and leading me through the warm kitchen to the settee where they slept. "Look at what your sister's done. Won't they know Father Christmas has been when they wake up!"

With her Junior Hair-Styler's scissors my sister had virtually scalped Uncle Kevin and my dad as they slept, and in the patchy tufts of hair she hadn't hacked off, she had rolled Junior Hair-Styler's curlers, all tightly gripped. They both had been given a full make-over too, complete with eye-liner, blusher and lipstick and, sitting on a damp patch on Uncle Kevin's knee, looking like a third ugly sister, was the dolly that couldn't stop weeing, also scalped and with lipstick applied with what looked like marker pen.

I looked down at the three piles of different coloured hair; ginger, brown and bleached blonde and up at my mum's face and I began to laugh. And as I began to laugh I began to cry, cold shudders of release pulling my shoulders until the Christmas tree lights became genies of liquid colour, in my eyes. I was glad I was home. And I knew that it all amounted to what we only ever need at Christmas time, now and always …

Love.

(Garry Burnett, A Yuletide Tale)

Discuss with your group and then your teacher the following topics:

- Christmas in your family – have you had any similar experiences?
- What made you laugh about the story – which were your favourite parts?
- Which parts made you sad?
- Did the boy cope well with the verbal bullying by his dad and Uncle Kevin?
- How could he have coped?

Written Follow-up

'Impulse-control'

The boy in the story ran away from home 'on impulse'. This means he did not really think through what could have happened to him when he did so. He did it 'on the spur of the moment'. Address the following in your written work:

1. Have you ever done anything 'without thinking' that, had you thought about it, you might never have done?
2. What could the boy in 'A Yuletide Tale' have done to cope with the situation?
3. What kinds of 'impulses' do people have that cause them to act without thinking?
4. Make a list of strategies for coping with your impulses. (For example, counting to ten before acting etc.)

'Self-awareness'; 'it's okay to cry'

Understanding our emotions is a key feature of emotional intelligence. Sometimes it is okay to cry and 'get the feelings out'. Sometimes, unfortunately, people are not sympathetic about other people expressing their emotions.

1. Why did the boy in 'A YuletideTale' want to cry in the first place?
2. How did he react to being teased?
3. What made the boy feel he couldn't cry?
4. How can we be better at allowing people to express their feelings?
5. Come up with a strategy for 'airing your feelings'.

6. How will you deal with emotions in the future?
7. Write an account of a time when you were so moved or upset by something that you cried.

Transfer

Be aware of your own feelings and reactions to people and situations and try to question yourself about why you feel as you do.

'Empathy'

The antidote or cure for insensitivity is 'empathy' or 'putting yourself in some-one else's shoes' in order to understand how they feel. Show your empathy for the boy in 'A Yuletide Tale' by writing him a reply to the following letter as if you were an 'Agony Aunt' (someone who answers problems on a 'problem page' in a newspaper or magazine). In your reply, give the boy advice on how to cope with similar situations in the future.

> Dear Aunt Sally,
>
> I'm fed up of being laughed at by my dad and my uncle. They always seem to pick on me and find things to put me down. What can you advise me to do? I often get so upset I lose my temper and do things on impulse I regret later.
>
> Angry of Hull

Write a letter to the author (Mr Burnett) reviewing the story. Are there any questions you would like to ask about any part of the story you didn't understand? Post these to:

Mr Burnett
Malet Lambert School Language College
James Reckitt Avenue
Hull
East Yorkshire HU8 0JD

'Put-downs' and 'Put-ups'

People often give us useful feedback on the way we have performed or behaved. A teacher might write "That was a good story, but I think you should have a bit more description in the opening paragraphs" on a piece of your writing.

Sometimes, however, feedback can be insensitively given and can come across as personal criticism. Sometimes we take criticism badly, even when it is offered with the best of intentions, i.e. to help us improve what we are doing.

A good guide is to 'never criticise the person, criticise the act': "That wasn't a very thoughtful thing you said because ..." would sound much better than "You are thoughtless" because you are criticising the *act*, not the *person*.

Or: "I didn't agree with the way you lost your temper then because ..." *rather than* "You are bad tempered".

People often use personal criticism to put other people 'down', usually in order to put themselves 'up'. Bullying of any kind, including verbal bullying, is something we should not tolerate.

Activities

1. Make your class a 'put-up zone' – design posters that illustrates this.
2. Come up with a set of class rules banning certain words and phrases. Try to find ways in your form of 'putting-up' people who have low self-esteem.
3. This is an ongoing activity. Try to praise someone every day. Make a real effort to congratulate someone on what they have done, on how they look, on something they have said etc. Avoid saying negative things that put others down.

'Optimism'

"They didn't love me". "Nobody loves me". Isn't it true that sometimes when we are angry with people or upset about something, suddenly everything seems bad? Being optimistic and resilient to setbacks is a crucial characteristic of a successful person. In other words, they never give in.

Read the following poem by Maya Angelou, 'Still I rise'. Maya Angelou has led a remarkable and rich life, full of challenges and setbacks but also full of achievement and excellence. And yet she refuses ever to let anything get her down.

Still I rise

You may write me down in history
with your bitter twisted lies
You may trod me in the very dirt
But still like dust I'll rise

Does my sassiness upset you?
Why are you beset with gloom?
'Cause I walk like I've got oil wells
Pumping in my living room

Just like the moons and like suns
With the certainty of tides
Just like hope springing high
Still I'll rise

Did you want to see me broken?
Bowed head and lowered eyes?
Shoulders falling like teardrops
Weakened by my soulful cries

Does my haughtiness offend you?
Don't take it awful hard
'Cause I laugh like I got goldmines
Diggin' in my back yard
You may shoot me with your words,
You may cut me with your eyes,
You may kill me with your hatefulness
But still, like air I'll rise

Does my sexiness upset you?
Does it come as a surprise
That I dance like I've got diamonds
At the meeting of my thighs?

Out of the huts of history's shame I rise
Up from a past that's rooted in pain I rise
I'm a black ocean, leaping and wide
Welling and swelling I bear in the tide

Leaving behind nights of terror and fear I rise
Into a daybreak that's wondrously clear I rise
Bringing the gifts that my ancestors gave
I am the dream and the hope of the slave
I rise, I rise, I rise …

(Maya Angelou)

Written follow-up

1. How does the narrator say she copes with the put-downs and negativity of others?
2. Choose examples from the poem to illustrate the narrator's 'optimism'.
3. Write an affirmation for how you will be emotionally intelligent with others.

Transfer and Generalisation

Positive thinking, 'optimism' and a sensitivity to the needs of others are important aspects of our 'personal' intelligence. Try to understand the reasons why you feel and react as you do – are they feelings that you can understand? Where did they come from? Are they justified? Are you being 'childish'? (Etc.) Affirm that you are a mature and thoughtful person who considers the needs and emotions of others. Your ability as a learner will grow as a result. Your intelligence as a person will be 'excellent'.

Chapter Ten
Evaluation and Transfer

Thinking You Can

Now that you have covered the first section of the 'Learning to Learn' course it is time to reflect on the power of this information, and of the attitudes and thinking that you have, to make positive changes to your life. When you connect all you have learnt about beliefs and attitudes with the information in Part Two on **Skills for Effective Learning** you will have the power to be able to direct and control your achievements in all sorts of remarkable ways.

Please try to put into writing what have been the important lessons for you from Part One and say how you have used them in your work and life to make positive changes to the way that you think and act.

The following should help focus your thinking:

1. What is the difference between 'intrinsic' and 'extrinsic' motivation?
2. What did you learn from Part One about the importance of having high self-esteem in learning?
3. Why did we do the 'join the dots' exercise?
4. What was interesting about the story of Cliff Young?
5. What is a 'comfort zone'? Why did we learn about these?
6. Write down three important ingredients of an 'affirmation'.
7. How is an affirmation different from a resolution?
8. Who did you benchmark in the benchmarking exercise? Why?
9. How did the story of 'Jack and the Storytelling Contest' link with Tiger Woods's affirmation "I smile at obstacles"?
10. What does SERIOUS stand for?
11. Re-read the poem 'Isn't it strange?' at the beginning of the book. How do you interpret this poem? How does it link to the kind of work you have done in *Learning to Learn*?
12. How has the Part One of *Learning to Learn* helped you to become a better learner?

Looking Forward

Part Two will help you learn some of the skills and techniques that will enable you to learn effectively in any new situation and to achieve your goals and affirmations.

Skills for
Effective Learning

Chapter Eleven
A Cage With Stout Bars?

The Red Cockatoo
Sent as a present from Annam
A Red Cockatoo
Coloured like the peach blossom
Speaking with the speech of men
And they did what they always do
To the learned and the eloquent
They took a cage with stout bars
And they shut it up inside.

(Po Chu'I, 8th century, translated by Arthur Waley)

Thinking About Learning

Kinds of Learning: 'KUS'

Knowledge   –   Memorising something
Understanding –   Concepts
Skills   –   Doing something

In pairs, try to categorise the following learning experiences into one of the three kinds of learning in the table. For each learning experience, place a tick in the column that most applies to it – i.e. under the kind of learning that you would use to learn that particular experience.

For example, if you think that learning the number of days in a year is mostly a 'memorising' exercise, then place a tick in that column.

Discuss each learning experience with your partner first. Some might fit into more than one column!

What does this tell us about the kind of learning that takes place in the many different subjects we study at school?

You should work in pairs and discuss your answers.

LEARNING EXPERIENCE	K	U	S
1. The number of days in a year			
2. How to make a spaghetti bolognese			
3. Why Henry VIII dissolved the monasteries			
4. The names of nine Roman Emperors			
5. The date of the first manned landing on the moon			
6. How to play badminton correctly			
7. How to read a map			
8. The causes of the First World War			
9. How to give an effective public speech			
10. Why the Catholics wanted to get rid of the Cathars in France			
11. The name of England's last ten prime ministers			
12. Why *The Simpsons* is a popular TV programme			
13. The names of the kings and queens of England			
14. How to play the piano			
15. The history of Blues music in the USA			

Questions

Now answer these questions in your exercise book:

1. How many of these experiences involved ticking more than one category?
2. What does this tell us about different types of learning?
3. Do you think there is a most 'important' kind of learning? If so, what is it? Why do you think so?
4. Which kind of learning would you say is the easiest for you?
5. Which kind of learning would you say is the most difficult for you?
6. Do you think different kinds of learning require different approaches and skills? What are they?

Thinking About Teaching

Mr Gorman or Miss Creedle?

You will first read a story called 'Mr Gorman', in which the writer remembers some very positive and negative early experiences of learning that he has had.
The story is also contained on the audio CD.

Mr Gorman

Mr Padley was our Headmaster when I started Southcoates Lane Junior Boys' School and I suppose the best way of describing him would be to say that he was like everybody's grandad. He seemed quite old to me, a boy of eight, at the time – the hair had disappeared from the top and back of his head and the sides were always neatly Brylcreamed back. He had a chubby pink face and wore thick glasses that can't have worked very well because he didn't seem to be able to see past the first three rows of the assembly hall. It never seemed to bother him if we swayed in time to the hymn or, occasionally, when Mr Canon, who played the piano, reminded Whincup, his page turner, to "get a flaming move on". In fact I think he found it all quite funny. And now when I try to think of him I get a picture of Captain Mainwaring from *Dad's Army* in my mind and I'm never sure which is which.

But he always made me feel he cared for the boys in his school, as if they were his own. '*His*' school. I always thought of it as *his* school, the same way I did my house to be *my* house. For some reason I couldn't imagine him anywhere but there and I was shocked out of my skin to see him eating an ice cream on the promenade at Bridlington one day. I almost hid in embarrassment.

When our teacher was off poorly, Mr Padley would sometimes stand in and take the lesson. He was a wonderful story-teller and had a large repertoire of 'voices' which he would use to bring them to life. Doing plays was best because he would say, "Who would like to play the part of …?" and before he'd finished everyone's hand would go up. "No one?" he would say, feigning astonishment, "Oh well, I'll have to do that one then." And he would end up doing every character in the play, each with a different voice, and we would sit back and listen and laugh.

Sometimes in assembly he would read out an article from the newspaper or tell us about somebody who had had something awful happen to them and we would squeeze our eyes shut while he said a special prayer. And I remember the day of the Aberfan disaster in Wales, when a mountain of coal debris slipped and engulfed a tiny school, killing many of its children and teachers, and Mr Padley stood and dabbed his eyes with his handkerchief as he told us all about it in a special assembly before reading a poem to remember the dead. I gave my dinner money to the collection.

So when Mrs Johnson came in one day to tell us that she had some very sad news and that Mr Padley had died unexpectedly during the night, we all felt the loss as if it were a member of our own family. The shiny black funeral cars drove slowly past the school and we all lined up on Southcoates Lane to sing 'For Those in Peril on the Sea', the school hymn, joined by hundreds of ex-pupils and parents. I don't think I'd seen so many people gathered in that way until the Queen came to Hull some time later. There were lots of people crying.

On the first day back the following September the floor in the hall shone like glass, and the warm smell of varnish and fresh paint made me feel quite faint as we all filed into our first assembly – wearing blazers and haircuts and stiff new shoes. All of a sudden the doors to the stairs burst open and in strode a very serious looking dark-haired man. He stood grimly holding on to the lectern without speaking as he raked the faces of the assembled boys with his glare, pulling down, row by row, the corners of every smile, until there was a hushed gloom in the hall.

"Good morning. Welcome back to the first day of your new term," he said. "My name is Mr Gorman and I am your new … Headmaster."

Then he suddenly yelled at the top of his voice at a boy in the third row.

"*You boy!* Is your mother *mental*?"

"Sir who me sir? No sir."

"Is your father *mental*?"

"No sir."

"Then why are you *mental*?"

"Sir I don't know sir."

"Anybody who talks when I am has got to be *mental*. Come out here!"

"Sir I wa'nt, honest!"

The boy mounted the stage and Mr Gorman held up what looked like a child's cricket bat with writing all over it. In fact it said, "Heat for the Seat" and there was a little picture of a boy with a glowing red bottom who'd just received it.

"Bend over!" commanded Mr Gorman and then he belted the unsuspecting boy on his bottom with the bat as if he were hitting him for six.

Next day Charlie Borrill, a chubby boy with sticking-up ginger hair, was summoned to the front after there was a bit of commotion around him.

"And you are?" he snapped at the quivering boy.

"I'm what, sir?"

"Don't try to be funny with me. Your name you idiot. What's your name, boy?"

"Sir Borrill"

"*Sir* Borrill, eh? When did you receive your knighthood?"

"Sir I don't know sir."

"Well, come on, boy, tell us all the joke so we can all enjoy the fun."

"Sir … sir. Sir," he croaked, going very red with embarrassment, "I made wind."

Despite being honest and genuinely sorry, Borrill was given two belts from 'Heat for the Seat' and ordered to see a 'vet' for acting in an unchristian manner during an act of worship.

Over the next few weeks he terrorised us all into gloomy silence and it appeared that everyone was at some stage going to be the focus of his attention. One day after sitting my test to see what grade I would take with me to 'big school' I was told by Mr Abram my form tutor that Mr Gorman wished to see me in his office. The loud tick of the school clock was nothing compared to the thumping of my heart in my throat as I lingered outside waiting to go in. I could hear his secretary tapping away at the typewriter in his room. A boy who "couldn't keep still" in his classroom had been sellotaped by the wrists to the corridor wall. If he moved and broke the tape, he had been warned, he would receive 'Heat for the Seat'.

"Come!" yelled Mr Gorman at my feeble knock.

"Sir, you wanted to see me," I croaked.

"And you are?"

"Burnett, Sir."

"Ah, yes," he said through thick spectacles, which magnified his eyes to menacing proportions, and he held up my examination paper in his hand. One of the questions on the paper had been "Find as many words as you can in 'TIME'." Simply by arranging all four letters I had written "MITE", "ITEM" and "EMIT".

"And how does a boy of ten know a word like 'emit' if he didn't cheat?" he sneered.

I had recently read a book on UFOs that described the noise a flying saucer had "emitted" and I'd had to look it up in the dictionary to find out what it meant. I'd swear there was a look of disappointment on his face when I offered this explanation and he never once said he was sorry.

Late one dark afternoon in February we were called into the hall for a "special assembly" and every boy shivered in nervous contemplation of their weekends' misdemeanours. Mr Gorman was already at the front of the hall, part-silhouetted against the window, and I tried not to look as great bruise-coloured clouds gathered behind him over the Humber. For a long time after we had all arrived he still didn't move.

"Sit," he said in a low voice. "David Valentine, remain standing."

Valentine was from a poor family. There was, it seemed, a Valentine in every year, and they all smelt of stale biscuits.

"Right, gentlemen," said Mr Gorman conspiratorially. "We have before us … a thief. This villain has been taking money from your coat pockets and today I am going to teach him and you a lesson that you'll never forget. Now then, lad, put on your spectacles."

Nobody knew that Valentine should have been wearing spectacles. In those days there wasn't the vast choice of nice frames that you can get nowadays and not many people could have afforded them anyway. You could either look like Buddy Holly or John Lennon and that was it. David Valentine, so often the object of scorn for his shabby clothes and shoes, was obviously too proud to endure the jeers of his schoolmates for spectacles and had never once had them on in class.

"I ant gor um wi' me sir."

"Oh," said Mr Gorman, feigning surprise, "it's a good job I went home for them, isn't it?" And out of his pocket he drew the spectacles like a conjuror producing the magic card at the end of the trick.

"Come and put them on then," he snarled, "and lets see if they're working properly."

And then he made him face the hymn sheets on the wall. "And if you don't sing sweetly," he said, tapping his palm with a cricket bat, "then I've got something here that might help."

The clouds on the horizon could have been foothills of distant mountains or dust clouds scuffed up from stampedes of wild beasts fast approaching as Mr Cannon struck the introductory chord for 'To be a Pilgrim' and David Valentine stood, his face crimson with shame, without making a single sound. After the second and third false starts to the hymn, the first tears spilled on to the boy's burning face. He was already broken, humiliated and we all cowered in anticipation of what was to come. The sound he made after he'd received the first stroke was like no other I've heard before or since. After the swift crack of wood on flesh he "keeed" in pain, and then again. After the third he collapsed sobbing on to the platform, a dark maroon stain seeping into the grey flannel of his shorts.

I didn't see Mr Gorman for nearly twenty years after I'd left. I was in Sainsbury's supermarket with my little girl. I handed her the shopping and she placed it carefully into the wire compartment at the front before I spun the trolley around like a waltzer car with her inside it. "Weeee …" She would chuckle before I grabbed the handle to stop it from crashing into the displays.

And suddenly he came around the corner of the aisle, holding on to a trolley himself. He seemed much smaller and thinner than I remembered and judging by the pull on the corner of his mouth he had suffered a stroke and held on to its handle as if for support.

I felt I ought to at least show him the courtesy of telling him who I was.

"Oh yes," he said faintly, not really remembering, "weren't you …?" And a thin string of saliva trickled down the side of his mouth. "Weren't you …?"

I felt like saying "The boy of ten you were about to beat for cheating because he'd merely taken the trouble to learn a word that he didn't understand. The boy of ten who had stood and watched helplessly while you bullied and intimidated and destroyed the love of learning that was in us all."

But I couldn't find the words … and neither could he.

How many words can you find in time? How many?

I chilled as he stroked my daughter's chin and then nodded and wished him well. But he died just two weeks later and I saw his obituary in the paper, which gave details of how much he had 'left' in his estate.

My goodness. To all those who'd been at his many lessons, it must seem like he'd left a great deal more.

(Garry Burnett, *Mr Gorman*)

You will now read a poem by Gareth Owen, called 'Miss Creedle Teaches Creative Writing', in which a boy recounts his experience of a lesson in creative writing led by a well-meaning teacher.

Miss Creedle Teaches Creative Writing

"This morning" cries Miss Creedle
"We're all going to use our imaginations,
We're going to close our eyes 3W and imagine.
Are we ready to imagine Darren?
I'm going to count to three.
At one we wipe our brains completely clean;
At two we close our eyes;
And at three, we imagine.
Are we all imagining? Good.
Here is a piece of music by Beethoven to help us.
Beethoven's dates were 1770 to 1827.
(See The Age of Revolutions in your History books.)
Although Beethoven was deaf and a German
He wrote many wonderful symphonies,
But this was a long time before anyone was born.
Are you imagining a time before you were born?
What does it look like? Is it dark?
(Embryo is a good word you might use.)
Does the music carry you away like a river?
What is the name of that river? Can you smell it?
'Foetid' is an exciting adjective.
As you float down the river
Perhaps you land on an alien planet.
Tell me what sounds you hear.
If there are indescribable monsters
Tell me what they look like but not now.
(Your book entitled Tackle Pre-history This Way
Will be of assistance here.)
Perhaps you are cast adrift in a broken barrel
In stormy shark-infested waters
(Remember the work we did on piranhas for RE?)
Try to see yourself. Can you do that?
See yourself at the bottom of a pothole in the Andes
With both legs broken
And your life ebbing away inexorably.
What does the limestone feel like?
See the colours
Have you done that? Good.
And now you may open your eyes.
Your imagining time is over,
Now it is writing time.
Are we ready to write? Good.

Then write away.
Wayne you're getting some exciting ideas down.
Tracy that's lovely.
Darren you haven't written anything.
Couldn't you put the date?
You can't think of anything to write.
Well what did you see when you closed your eyes?
But you must have seen something beside the black.
Yes apart from the little squiggles.
Just the black. I see.
Well try to think
Of as many words for black as you can."

Miss Creedle whirls about the class like a benign typhoon
Spinning from one quailing homestead to another.
I dream of peaceful ancient days
In Mr Swindell's class
When the hours pass like a dream
Filled with order and measuring and tests.

Excitement is not one of the things I come to school for.
I force my eyes shut, kicking ineffectually at the starter
But all I see
Is a boy of twelve
Sitting at a desk one dark November day
Writing this poem.
And Darren is happy to discover
There is only one word for black
And that will have to suffice
Until the bell rings for all of us.

(Gareth Owen, from *Song of the City*)

After reading these accounts, answer the following questions and complete the activities.

Questions

1. Why does the boy in the story 'Mr Gorman' prefer Mr Padley to Mr Gorman?
2. What does Mr Gorman say and do that makes him so frightening to the boys?
3. In what ways is Miss Creedle a good teacher? Give reasons for your opinions. How could she improve her teaching style?

Activities

1. Write a job description for your ideal teacher. This can be as long and as detailed as you like. Imagine that this was going to form part of an advertisement for a teacher to be placed in the educational press. List the qualities you would expect that teacher to have.
2. Write a description of two very good teachers you have known. Try to describe them in detail (not just what they looked like) and give examples of things they said and did that made them good teachers.

Transfer and Generalisation

- How can a teacher make learning easier for you in any subject?
- When is it easiest for you to learn?
- When is it more difficult?
- How would it be if you had a choice about or control over the way you learn?

On the last point, here is an example to help you decide.

If I were to say, "We will study Shakespeare next term and the work you do will involve:

- watching videos and a live production of the play, or
- reading it aloud around the class, or
- acting the play out in order to understand it fully"

would you have a preference? Think about what that preference might be and why.

By completing the work in Part Two, you should be able to discover good reasons why this is so.

Chapter Twelve
Your Remarkable Brain

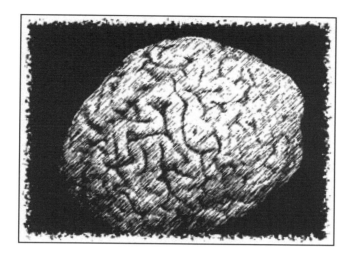

Scientists have called it the most complex organism in the universe: the human brain. But if you were to look at a human brain you would probably think it was nothing special.

Touch it and you might be surprised at how soft it is, all wrinkly like a walnut on the outer surface, with a consistency a bit like cottage cheese, and yet it is responsible for all of our thoughts, feelings, intelligence and memories, and for making each of us the person we are.

There are some remarkable qualities to this unique part of our body that we can only marvel at. It has seemingly unlimited ability to learn, to memorise and be creative, and it possesses an intricate inner-working system so complex that scientists feel they are only just beginning to understand it.

Phrenology

Only one hundred and fifty years ago people believed that a person's character and abilities could be measured by the size of different parts of their brain and the bumps on their scalps that corresponded to them. This was the 'science' of phrenology, developed by Franz Gall, which was quickly undermined when serious research began to discover far more complex organisation in the brain, connected with how language was produced and how brain damage could affect different functions and capabilities.

As our medical and technological capabilities advanced, so did our ability to understand how different parts of the brain are responsible for different functions.

In the twentieth century, technology began to be developed that would allow scientists to look at living brains and to observe, amid all of the mass complexity of activity, how we use specific areas of our brains to do different things.

How Can Knowing Information About Our Brains Help Us to Become Better Learners?

No 'user's guide' or accelerated learning programme can give us a complete insight into the brain. There are, however, certain findings that neuroscientists share that can help us understand how to work *with* our brains to become more effective learners. This information is being updated all the time as new research findings are debated and published.

Physical Facts About Your Brain

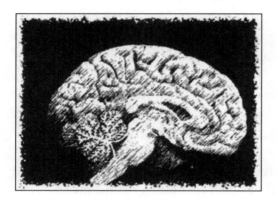

Your brain has two halves called 'hemispheres'. Each has different jobs to do that are connected with thinking and learning and making your body work efficiently. The two hemispheres are joined in the middle by a bundle of nerves called the 'corpus callosum' and these act as telephone lines between the two hemispheres. Messages from your brain are then carried to your body along nerves through the spinal cord.

It is believed that the right and left areas of the brain have the following responsibilities:

Left cerebral hemisphere	**Right cerebral hemisphere**
Language	Music
Numbers	Images, pictures
Symbols and codes	Artistic creativity
Facts, details	Daydreaming
Linear (step-by-step) processes	Big picture, meaning

New research is showing that although this is broadly true, there is actually a lot more to it than that and, for example, when a person sings a song, or hums the tune, or reads the lyrics, there is considerable crossover as both hemispheres of the brain are activated.

The Triune Brain Theory

An American scientist called Paul McLean devised a popular theory called the 'triune brain theory', in which he described the brain as working on three different levels, all interlinked (see also the first section of the 'Family Learning Pack' video):

1. The Reptilian Brain

The oldest part of our brain is often called the 'reptilian' brain because in the course of evolution this was the first part of our brain to develop, and a part of the brain we share with all animals. It is also the part of our brain that is responsible for keeping our life-support systems going, for looking after us and protecting us when we are under threat. In times of stress or when we are in danger it releases chemicals into our bloodstream that affect the way we feel and so makes us more aware of keeping safe and protecting ourselves.

Some of these chemicals, such as adrenaline, make our muscles work more efficiently and therefore make us more able to fight a potential enemy or run away.

If we are constantly living in an atmosphere of stress or if relaxing is difficult then it is likely that we will find learning new things very difficult. Our memories will be less efficient and our ability to concentrate and solve problems limited. Our main priority will be our own well-being. This is because quite literally the first message coming from the 'reptilian' brain will be "Survive!" New learning will take *second* place.

The main conclusion we should draw from this is the importance of relaxation, self-esteem and confidence.

All of the work you did on self-esteem and confidence building from Part One will help dispel typical reptilian brain states, which involve anxiety, stress and low confidence.

More on this in a little while.

2. The Emotional/Limbic Brain

As human beings evolved through time they began to develop more complex emotional responses. They learned to have friends and enemies, how to laugh and cry, and how to love and grieve.

Emotional responses and a large part of our emotional intelligence are conducted by activity generated in this part of the brain.

The limbic centre, the 'amygdala', generates most of our emotional responses to the world around us.

From the point of view of 'learning', the most interesting thing about the limbic centre is its closeness to the area of the brain that forms long-term memories.

Think of how many of your strongest memories have an emotion attached to them (birthdays, happy holidays, Christmas, family bereavements etc.). A strong positive emotion will cement a memory into place. Humour, surprise, novelty, even rudeness can all be used to enhance memories and make them stronger!

Also situated in the limbic area is a part of the brain called the 'reticular formation'.

The reticular formation (RF)

This is a device we possess that helps us to decide what is most important to us at a particular point in time. It creates priorities for action and for the storage and retrieval of important information.

Imagine having your own secretary who sorted out all of your school bag, threw away all the junk and only allowed you to take what you needed for school that day (I know for most of you that person is possibly called a 'mum' or 'dad'!). This is what the reticular formation does; it allows in only the most important information for our attention – the rest it marginalises or even ignores. Otherwise the brain would be bombarded with information and would not know which way to turn!

A good example of this would be for me to say "think of your feet". Until they were mentioned, I'm sure not many of you were thinking of your feet. Now it is likely that you can't stop noticing them because the reticular formation has increased your awareness of them.

Try quickly reading these two phrases:

 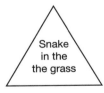

Until we are alerted to excess information by our reticular formation, our brain will only process the information it needs to make sense or gain a complete picture of understanding – and sometimes it will cut corners or even deceive us as to the truth.

Both of the triangles have two "the"s in them: "Paris in the the spring" and "Snake in the the grass". The extra "the" was possibly seen as excess information and as getting in the way of those phrases making sense. Physically, within our brains, we are instinctively trying to find a match to some other familiar information, and to connect that information with what we already know. We have probably already heard the phrase "Paris in the spring" so it is easy for us to make the match; the extra information ("the the") does not match the picture we have and so our brains tell us to ignore it.

3. The Neo-Cortex

The main function of the neo-cortex is to help us understand the world by connecting together what we experience and what we already know.

In order to begin doing this, the neo-cortex likes to have the 'big picture', or big idea, of what is happening and does not like to be hampered by the stressful interruptions of chemicals coming from the reptilian brain.

Once we are able to see the big picture and how it fits in with the work we are doing, we can work towards the end result more purposefully as our neo-cortex becomes busy finding answers and connections that will be useful along the way.

Remember times when you have tried to understand something by saying, "Is it like ...?". This is your brain trying to get a 'big picture' of what the new information means by linking it to something you already know.

Novelty, fun and learning styles

The brain is excited by new experiences and soon bored by repetition. Novelty or 'newness' means new brain activity. Trying to do things 'differently' will often mean a much more interesting and successful learning experience.

We also like, above all else, learning to be 'fun'. Not necessarily 'funny', in the sense that it makes us laugh all the time, but interesting and exciting, giving us pleasure in discovery and achievement.

The brain also connects the way we learn something with the information being learned. If the experience of learning is a successful and pleasurable one, then the brain will associate, or connect together, those feelings with the learning experience.

Because of this, it is possible to develop a 'preferred' learning style, which represents the favourite way of learning we have developed. That 'preferred' way of learning might use 'kinesthetic' (or activity-based), visual (sight-based) or auditory (sound-based) methods. (More on this later in the book.)

For this reason, the neo-cortex is sometimes called the 'association cortex'. It learns and remembers by connecting and linking information by association. (More on 'connections' following the next section.)

Brain cells (neurons, axons and dendrites)

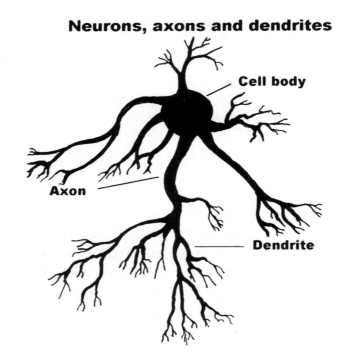

Neurons, axons and dendrites

Cell body

Axon

Dendrite

The outer tissue of the neo-cortex, which looks so wrinkled and convoluted, is made up of billions of brain cells called 'neurons'.

These cells are responsible for recording all of the things we learn, and their job is to try to connect what we learn with other information already stored in the brain.

So, if I were to start by describing a neuron as looking "a little bit like a starfish in shape", you would search in your knowledge of starfish shapes for a connection and gain an idea of what a neuron looks like by connecting the two.

Every time we perceive something with our senses, the neuron records the experience by growing a branch from the cell body called an 'axon'. The job of the axon is to make contact with other networks that hold similar information and to connect with them using little terminals called 'dendrites'. The purpose of this activity is to help us create an understanding of the new information by connecting with something we have already 'assimilated' or understood.

Connections in the brain (synapses)

Q. Why is an exercise book like a lazy dog?
A. Because an exercise book has an *ink-lined* page …
   and an *inclined* page is a *slope up* …
   and a *slow pup* is a *lazy dog*!

From autopsies of the brains of foetuses and people ranging in age from a few months to their nineties, scientists have measured samples of brain tissue about the size of a pinhead, each containing about 70,000 brain cells.

In a sample from a 28-week-old foetus, one scientist found 124 million connections (called 'synapses') between the cells. The same size sample in a newborn baby had 253 million connections, and in an 8-month-old the number had exploded to 572 million.

At the fastest rate, connections are being built at the incredible speed of 3 billion per second, eventually reaching a total of about 1,000 trillion connections in the whole brain. It is not the *number* of brain cells or the size of our brains that helps make us intelligent but the complexity of *connections* that are made between them. The more connections there are and the more ways the connections are made makes a significant difference to our 'intelligence', resourcefulness and ability to solve problems. This is because we are able to see comparisons and links, connect different ideas and see similarities between different kinds of problem. And of course we also make connections by linking information to ideas that we have already experienced.

In the plenaries at the end of your 'Learning to Learn' lesson you should be looking for how what you have learnt is similar or connected to other work you have done. You should always be looking for an opportunity to use what you have learnt in another subject or lesson.

Gestalt

So how can we put this to use? How can we make this function work to our advantage in helping us to become better and more effective learners?

The psychologist Max Wertheimer was among a group of thinkers who devised a theory called 'gestalt' psychology. This group believed that human beings are constantly looking for 'completeness' – for things to be finished and whole – and constantly looking for patterns of meaning and order. Until they find the match, or if something stands in the way of them completing something, they will go to great lengths to finish off the job – even to the point of cutting corners or leaving out words – so that the meaning will be complete.

Remember how irritating it was the last time you could not remember the name of that film star or pop star? Remember how it nagged you? And how good it felt when you did finally remember?

This is one good reason why you should never check your own work! The brain will make short cuts to complete the picture and leave things out or even add things in. We are so driven to 'make sense' by our brains that we will even go on unconsciously thinking and solving problems in our sleep. Who has woken up to remember where they left those keys or the answer to that homework problem?

Gestalt and affirmations

Hence the power of our affirmations. If we constantly make a picture in our minds of ourselves as better, more capable, stronger, more confident than we are now, then, as our belief system starts to transform, the 'gestalt' will help us look very creatively and with great determination for ways of making the affirmation come true. 'Gestalt' will give us the energy to search for ways of completing the picture and suddenly we will start noticing people and things that can help us in our goal.

Treat each of your affirmations as a kind of *scavenger hunt*. Remember the boy in the story of 'The Mile'? Once he had made the affirmation that he would beat Arthur Boocock in the mile race, nothing else mattered and he looked for every opportunity to train and prepare for the race.

Activity

In groups of three or four, one person picks a letter from the alphabet and calls it out. The others write down five things they can see that begin with that letter. Swap until everyone has had a turn at picking a letter.

Notice how you suddenly become aware of things around you that did not matter before you began the activity.

Questions

1. What is the reticular formation?
2. How can it help us to become better learners?

Scavenger Hunt: let's put our RF to work!

Congratulations on finding:

In school
1. A teacher wearing a red tie
2. Someone carrying a Manchester United bag
3. A car with a baby seat in
4. Two sets of twins in a different year from your own
5. Three teachers with black shoes

6. A broken window
7. A teacher who is left-handed
8. Three people with the same hairstyle
9. Five rooms with at least one plant in
10. Two places you can get a drink of water

Elsewhere
1. Three houses for sale
2. Five satellite TV dishes
3. A house called after someone's name
4. A cat or dog sitting in someone's window
5. A piece of garden furniture
6. Someone delivering things
7. A burglar alarm
8. Two telephone boxes
9. A post box
10. A sign saying, "Beware of the dog!"
11. A house with a skip outside it
12. A dog in a car
13. Clothes hanging out to dry
14. A triangular road sign
15. A police vehicle

Again, notice how quickly you become more alert and start looking for the things on these lists, whereas before they probably did not matter as much.

In order to fulfil our affirmations we need to be *resourceful,* which means keeping our eyes open for anything that will help us achieve them.

Transfer

- Be a learning scavenger. Scavenge for ideas and information.
- Talk to people who have already been through the processes you are going through, read books, benchmark the gifted and open up your RF to the important information that will allow you to complete your goals.

Plasticity and Enrichment

One final word, and remember – although this information is a summary of some very serious research by neuroscientists, it is a broad generalisation of how our brains work.

One of the most exciting discoveries about the human brain is that it has a quality that scientists call 'plasticity'. This means that the brain can actually re-programme itself to learn things if an area becomes damaged or even lost. Plasticity shows us how the brain can adapt to changes in the environment and reflect the state of things around it. If the environment is enriched and interesting then our brains will become enriched, interested and efficient at working in that environment. If the environment is dull, uninspiring and boring then our brains will be bored and uninspired.

This was never proved more effectively than in a study made of rats and their responses to a scientific test to see how they responded to 'enrichment'. Two sets of rats were placed in cages where they had identical amounts of space to move around in, but one cage was full of challenges such as mazes and toys. The result was that those rats in the enriched environment had many more connections in their brains than those in the unenriched environment.

Transfer

The lesson for us all is to surround ourselves with books, videos, information, and to make visits and seek experiences that will enrich the topics we study.

Intelligence can be increased by 'multiple' forms of experience. (More on this in the next section.)

Food for Thought: Ten Key Brain Bytes

1. Every brain is an intelligent, individual, biological organism. No two brains are the same.
2. Our brains have a quality called 'plasticity', which means they constantly change and grow according to the stimulation they receive.
3. Relaxation and 'composure' is a critical state of mind for learning.
4. Music can aid in creating an appropriate state of mind for learning.
5. Oxygen is crucial to brain functioning. Lots of fresh air!
6. Drink lots of water – dehydration causes loss of concentration.
7. Sleep cements learning and makes us alert.
8. Emotion is a key to forming long-term memories.
9. Connections and multiple 'representations' matter more than numbers of brain cells.
10. Every brain is a beautifully sophisticated, unique and miraculous work of creation. Treasure yours!

Your Remarkable Brain: Activities

1. You are considered to be a leading expert on the brain and learning and you are attending an important conference where you have been asked to deliver a 5-minute opening address on 'Recent understanding of the brain and learning'. Prepare your speech using the information in this book and any other research you have made yourself.
2. Write and illustrate a pamphlet for Year 6 pupils entitled 'Interesting and important things you should know about your brain'.
3. Draw a cartoon entitled 'A day in the life of a typical human brain'. Use it as a humorous way of explaining to someone younger than you about some of this important new information and ideas.
4. Play 'Who Wants to be a Millionaire?' (following). Using the information here, devise a series of questions for your class or another class that will test their knowledge of information about the brain.

Who Wants to be a Millionaire?

Using the information on the brain given on the previous pages and in the 'Learning to Learn' video, make a list of 15 questions (each with four possible answers) all about the brain.

Test each other with them. For example:

> **1.** The human brain is divided into two halves. These halves are called:
>
> **A.** Stratospheres **B.** Atmospheres **C.** Hemingways **D.** Hemispheres

1. _____
A. _____ B. _____ C. _____ D. _____

£100

2. _____
A. _____ B. _____ C. _____ D. _____

£200

3. _____
A. _____ B. _____ C. _____ D. _____

£300

4. _____
A. _____ B. _____ C. _____ D. _____

£500

5. _____
A. _____ B. _____ C. _____ D. _____

£1,000

6. _____
A. _____ B. _____ C. _____ D. _____

£2,000

7. _____
A. _____ B. _____ C. _____ D. _____

£4,000

8. _____
A. _____ B. _____ C. _____ D. _____

£8,000

9. _____
A. _____ B. _____ C. _____ D. _____

£16,000

10. _____
A. _____ B. _____ C. _____ D. _____

£32,000

11. _____
A. _____ B. _____ C. _____ D. _____

£64,000

12. _____
A. _____ B. _____ C. _____ D. _____

£125,000

13. _____
A. _____ B. _____ C. _____ D. _____

£250,000

14. _____
A. _____ B. _____ C. _____ D. _____

£500,000

15. _____
A. _____ B. _____ C. _____ D. _____

£1,000,000

*Mindmapping**

A Picture Paints a Thousand Words

What do you connect or associate with each of these pictures?

1. _____
_____
_____
_____

2. _____
_____
_____

3. _____
_____
_____

4. _____
_____
_____

5. _____
_____
_____

6. _____
_____
_____

7. _____
_____
_____
_____

8. _____
_____
_____

9. _____
_____
_____

10. _____
_____
_____
_____

Write what you think each of these pictures symbolises or 'stands for'. For example, the lion stands for *courage* and *strength* and is considered to be *the king of the jungle beasts*.

*Mind Maps® is a registered Trade Mark of The Buzan Organisation

What is Mindmapping?

(See also the 'Learning to Learn' video.)

Mindmapping is a great way of working with the natural way your brain connects and understands new information. It was invented by Tony Buzan, who is an international expert on memory and learning.

Mindmapping is a very powerful way of increasing your ability to learn effectively and quickly.

How to Make a Mindmap

You will need some felt-tip pens in lots of different colours and a large sheet of plain A3 paper.

Step 1

Turn the paper on its side and write the central idea in the middle of the paper. Use at least three different colours for this section of your Mindmap and include a picture or symbol of what the idea is.

For example, if you are going to produce a Mindmap on the topic of 'Learning to Learn' then draw the central symbol or image you associate with it in the centre of the paper. In this case it should be something that stands for 'Learning to Learn'. It could be a brain, for example, or somebody winning a race. I have chosen a *head*.

Step 2

Then draw some bold branches leading from the central image. Along each one write the main ideas that lead off from the central idea. The branches should be the same length as the main idea and each of the branches should be a different colour.

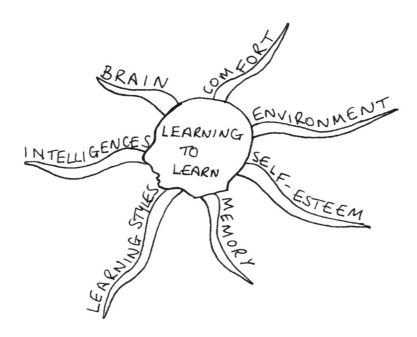

Step 3

Draw smaller branches leading from the main point. These are for connected, but less important, ideas. Use symbols, pictures, codes and shorthand in your Mindmaps in order to make them very personal, and add colour and imagery to the picture.

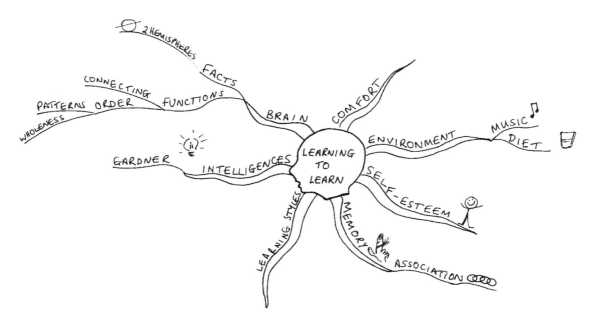

As you decipher these it will help you to remember what you are learning. Ideas will probably keep occurring to you and you must add them to the Mindmap on the appropriate branches.

Have you noticed how much like the shape of a 'neuron' the Mindmap is becoming?

Remember, Mindmaps can be about anything.

Activity

Produce your own Mindmap of any of the following topics:

- A topic covered in one of your subjects last term
- The front page of your local newspaper
- The human brain
- Multiple Intelligence
- Myself

Chapter Thirteen

Multiple Intelligences and Learning Styles

Five Things About Me

Call My Bluff

Think of five interesting and unusual things about you. These might be things you have achieved or things you are good at. They might be unusual or special things that you are interested in.

Four of the things must be true, but one of them must be a fib! Write them in this grid ready to share with the others in your group. Read them aloud to the group, each member of which then has to guess in turn which is the 'fib'.

The thing about me …	True/False

As you can see, we all have unique experiences, interests and talents. In this section we are going to explore how we can use these talents to become better learners.

Intelligence

Read the following accounts of different kinds of 'intelligence'. There are some short exercises to complete afterwards.

1. Mental Capacity

Intelligence is a very general mental capacity that, among other things, involves the ability to reason, plan, solve problems, think abstractly, comprehend complex ideas, learn quickly and learn from experience. It is not merely book learning, a narrow academic skill, or test-taking smarts. Rather, it reflects a broader and deeper capability for comprehending our surroundings – 'catching on', 'making sense' of things, or 'figuring out' what to do.

(John Carroll, *Wall Street Journal*, 13 December 1994)

2. 'Run, Forrest ...'

One of the funniest and most touching films to be made in America in the 1990s was the Oscar-winning movie *Forrest Gump*, starring Tom Hanks, based on the books by Winston Groome.

Early in his life Forrest is classed as having 'sub-normal' intelligence on the basis of his poor performance in IQ tests at school and, to add to his burdens, he is forced to wear 'leg-irons' by a doctor who believes that only by doing so will he straighten out his 'crooked' spine.

He is bullied by other boys and does not appear to have much going for him, except his friendship and love for his sweetheart Jenny, who protects him, encourages him and whom he eventually, towards the end of the film, marries.

Forrest discovers, almost by accident, that he can run very fast and he soon uses his ability to become a national college football star. Although he is classified as having sub-normal intelligence, Forrest seems to shine at all sorts of activities involving using his body and, after beating the army record for assembling a rifle and winning a congressional medal of honour for bravery as he runs his wounded comrades out of an ambush in Vietnam, Forrest goes on to be a national 'ping-pong' champion, representing America against China. He then becomes a shrimp fisherman, and, as with everything else he touches, makes an incredible success of it, accumulating a massive fortune and becoming a "go-zillionaire" businessman.

The film is meant to be satirical (making fun) about history and the way that people and things are not always as they seem. Forrest, without knowing it, plays a part in teaching Elvis Presley how to shake his hips in his famous pelvis dance and, supposedly, gives John Lennon the inspiration for his classic song 'Imagine'.

But Forrest displays two important qualities that we should note as we consider this section on intelligence and how it can take different shapes in different people.

First, Forrest is especially good at skills that are *kinesthetic* (of the body), and second, he never gives up – he shows *tenacity* and ultimately becomes a 'winner' in every sense.

Although Forrest is very strong on bodily-kinesthetic ability he does not do so well in other areas. For example, his people skills are not very good, his language and ability to use maths are limited and he does not seem to be very creative – he does not have many original ideas, or play a musical instrument, or write stories and poems or come up with fantastic scientific theories.

Yet many people would consider him to have very special intelligence. What do you think?

3. *Thomas Greene Bethune – 'Blind Tom'*

'Autism' is a special kind of mental condition that causes people who suffer from it to be very limited in their ability to cope with the world around them. Sometimes 'autistic' people can develop what has been termed 'savant syndrome'. Savants have highly specialised abilities, usually in a subject with very clear and 'circumspect' rules like Mathematics or Music, or they become incredibly good at reproducing photograph-like drawings and sculptures of objects and places they have seen. This is an account of a young savant boy who showed early signs of high musical intelligence.

Till he was five or six years old he could not speak, scarce walk, and gave no other sign of intelligence than his everlasting thirst for music, but at four years already, if taken out of the corner where he lay dejected, he would play beautiful tunes, his little hands having already taken possession of the keys, and his wonderful ear for any combination of notes they had only once heard.

Late one night Colonel Bethune, who had no idea of the boy's talent, heard music coming from the drawing room in the darkened house. Thinking that it must be one of his daughters playing, although that would be odd at such a late hour, he ventured downstairs and was startled to find the four year old blind boy, so limited in other ways, playing a Mozart sonata – without flourish or error. He had learned it by listening to it being played by the colonel's daughter, who had mastered it after weeks of practice. The colonel was astonished.

Like any slave child, Tom never attended school, and he was incapable of learning in areas other than music. He was relentless and explosive and required constant supervision. He seemed irresistibly drawn to the piano and within a few years, without any instruction whatsoever, he could listen to a piece of music once, then sit down at the piano and play it note for note, accent for accent and without error or interruption.

(Darrold A. Treffert, *Extraordinary People*)

4. Teaching Baldrick to Count

'Head'

Scene One: Blackadder's Lodgings

Blackadder is sitting at the table with Baldrick, who is looking perplexed.

BLACKADDER: Right, Baldrick, let us try again shall we? This is called adding. If I have two beans and then I add two more beans, what do I have?

Deep thought, then …

BALDRICK: Some beans.

BLACKADDER: Yes and no. Let's try again. If I have two beans and then I add two more beans, what does that make?

BALDRICK: *(More thought)* Ummm … a very small casserole?

BLACKADDER: Baldrick, the ape creatures of the Indus have mastered this. Now try again. One, two, three, four, so how many are there?

BALDRICK: Three.

BLACKADDER: What?

BALDRICK: And that one.

BLACKADDER: "Three and that one", so if I add that one to the three, what will I have?

BALDRICK: Some beans.

BLACKADDER: Yes. To you, Baldrick, the Renaissance was just something that happened to other people, wasn't it?

> (Richard Curtis, Ben Elton, John Lloyd and Rowan Atkinson, from
> *Blackadder II*, Episode 2, 'Head')

5. Homer Learns ICT

HOMER: *[reading screen]* "To Start, Press Any Key."

Where's the ANY key? I see Esk ["*ESC*"], Catarl ["*CTRL*"], and Pig-Up ["*PGUP*"].

There doesn't seem to be any *ANY* key.

Woo! All this computer hacking is making me thirsty.

I think I'll order a TAB. [*Presses TAB key.*]

> (Matt Groening, from *The Simpsons*, 3F05)

Discuss

- After reading these accounts, what is your definition of 'intelligence'?
- What does an 'intelligent' person do?
- How do you think 'savant' intelligence is different from 'traditional' human intelligence?

Activity

Make a list of the top five most intelligent people you can think of. Be prepared to share these with the rest of the class and to give reasons why you chose the people you did.

The Theory of Multiple Intelligences

In the 1980s Howard Gardner, a professor at Harvard University, changed the way that many of us thought about intelligence with his ground-breaking book *Frames of Mind*. In it he introduced his idea that people possess many different, 'multiple' intelligences (MI), and not just the ability to use words and numbers that is measured in the traditional IQ test. (IQ, which stands for 'intelligence quotient', is tested on how good you are at using language and numbers.)

Howard Gardner's definition of intelligence was that when someone could "make something" or "solve problems" that would be *valued* by the society they lived in, they were showing intelligence. This process can take many different forms. According to Gardner there are at least *nine ways* that you can show you are intelligent. They are:

Intelligence	This means ...
1. Linguistic	being talented at using and understanding words
2. Visual spatial	being talented at thinking in pictures and images
3. Musical	being talented at producing rhythms and melodies
4. Bodily kinesthetic	being talented at activities involving physical movement or touch
5. Logical mathematical	being talented at problem-solving with numbers and patterns
6. Interpersonal	being talented at understanding and working with people
7. Intrapersonal	being talented at understanding yourself and your deeper thoughts
8. Naturalist	being talented at understanding and working with nature
9. Existential	being talented at understanding religious and spiritual ideas

Gardner claims that we can use these many different 'intelligences' to be more thoughtful and effective learners in different situations and subjects at school.

What was so important about Gardner's theory was that it allowed us to acknowledge that people like Forrest Gump who do not have high IQs are intelligent in other, equally important, ways. In other words, there is a lot more diversity to intelligence than just being 'book smart'.

We will now deal with each of these intelligences in turn and try to build a better understanding of what they are and how you can use each of them to develop your mind and become a better all-round and effective learner.

CD Learning Styles: Intelligence Profile

First, you should complete the Multiple Intelligences programme to get some indication of what your profile is. The programme does not include questions to assess 'Naturalist' or 'Existential' intelligence.

Make a printout of your profile and stick it in your 'Learning to Learn' exercise book.

Discuss your profile with others and ways in which you think you could become a better 'all-rounder'.

1. LINGUISTIC Intelligence

"Cursive writing does not mean what I think it means"
(Bart Simpson)

This is the intelligence that is all about 'language'. Lawyers, poets, novelists, scriptwriters, journalists, comedians and all those who use language in their occupation usually have strong linguistic intelligence. They are good at using language to entertain, describe, persuade and instruct. They might be skilled at word-games, drama, improvisational comedy, talking or storytelling. They might be interested in foreign languages and find language learning relatively easy. All sorts of wordplay will fascinate them, as well as jokes, jingles, rhymes and puns.

Linguistic intelligence stars

(You might like to find out more about these people using the Internet.)

William Shakespeare, Dylan Thomas, Winston Churchill, J. K. Rowling, Richard Curtis, Ben Elton, Victoria Wood, Maureen Lipman, Maya Angelou

Ten ways to use or develop your linguistic intelligence

1. Play or devise word-games, anagrams, crosswords, Scrabble etc.
2. Use a library/bookshop/second-hand shop. Read at least one book a week.
3. Use one new word every day (vocabulary building). Start with 'ambivalent'.
4. Memorise a famous poem so that you could recite it aloud.
5. Listen to recordings of great readers performing 'classics' as a change from music.
6. Listen to good storytellers and try repeating their stories to your friends.
7. Get a thesaurus and use it regularly to improve your vocabulary.
8. Read a range of different writing (not just computer magazines or Harry Potter books, as good as they are!).
9. Keep a response journal and write your own reviews to films, books and CDs you have read, seen or listened to. Keep a diary for a month.
10. Try writing in the style of different writers, e.g. Dylan Thomas, Ernest Hemingway, Wendy Cope, Ted Hughes, Mark Twain, Harper Lee.

2. VISUAL SPATIAL Intelligence

This intelligence is the kind of talent that involves thinking in pictures and images. Film directors, artists, photographers, engineers, designers and architects are all people who excel in this intelligence. It involves being able to get a clear picture of things and to think through what something will look like and what sort of space it will fill. It also means that you are likely to respond to visually beautiful things and to create and interpret pictures with good attention to detail.

Visual-spatial intelligence stars

(You might like to find out more about these people using the Internet.)

Claude Monet, Steven Spielberg, Laura Ashley, Prince Charles, Laurence Llewelyn-Bowen, Barbara Hepworth, Emma Thompson, Sister Wendy, Salvador Dali

Ten ways to use or develop your visual-spatial intelligence

1. Visit an art gallery in order to 'read' and interpret narrative pictures.
2. Turn information into pictorial representations such as Mindmaps.
3. Develop a system of visual symbols you can use for note-taking.
4. Make a power-point presentation of a topic you have studied.
5. Study the ways visual images in films and TV programmes are composed (e.g. lighting and use of camera angles/shots).
6. Study optical illusions (see the work of Escher); create your own.
7. Design new inventions. Make prototype models.
8. Learn some simple origami.
9. Read maps and plot routes you have travelled, sites of historical events, places of interest etc.
10. Work on jigsaws, Rubik's cubes etc.

3. MUSICAL Intelligence

This is the ability to feel and produce musical sounds, rhythms and melodies. It is the talent to express feelings and ideas in the abstract form of music. People who possess this in great strength can 'hear' melodies and tunes in nature or in the environment. They can sing or play instruments tunefully from a very early age, or show appreciation for subtle interpretations of musical ideas by skilled performers. They are inspired and moved by music and often find themselves tapping rhythms or whistling or singing melodies.

Musical intelligence stars

(You might like to find out more about these people using the Internet.)

Eva Cassidy, Wolfgang Amadeus Mozart, Stevie Wonder, Gordon Giltrap, Blind Tom Bethune, Paul McCartney, Evelyn Glennie, Elton John, Lesley Garrett, Billie Holiday, Cat Stevens (Yusuf Islam)

Ten ways to use or develop your musical intelligence

1. Turn important information into lyrics to be sung to a well-known tune.
2. Have a week off listening to your favourite CDs. Listen to folk, jazz or blues!
3. Try to see how a great work of literature was transformed into a musical (e.g. *Les Miserables*).
4. Write extra verses to your favourite songs.
5. Hold a regular get-together music evening with friends where you take turns to introduce each other to a newly discovered CD track you like.
6. Select a series of 'inspirational' tunes and songs as a part of your personal portfolio. Make a tape with all of them on.
7. Choose music to reflect the mood or character of the work you are doing (e.g. for History, a suitable historical period piece). Play it while working.
8. Learn about musical prodigies and benchmark the methods they employed to become so successful (e.g. Mozart, Beethoven, Stevie Wonder).
9. Compose music or songs about the things you study.
10. Use jingles, raps and rhymes to record information in your memory.

4. BODILY KINESTHETIC Intelligence

This is the talent of our physical natures. Anything we do that involves touch or movement means that we have to use this aspect of our intelligence. Some possess it in great quantities: circus performers, sports men and women, dancers, martial artists, actors and actresses, craftsmen, footballers, mechanics – anybody who excels at active 'tactile' pursuits. To have this kind of intelligence is to have the sensitivity and ability to move our bodies with great co-ordination and flexibility, to show grace and control and to be able to perform physical routines or physical acts that require subtle and careful movements.

Bodily-kinesthetic intelligence stars/characters

(You might like to find out more about these people using the Internet.)

Bruce Lee, David Beckham, Harry Houdini, Julia Roberts, Dawn French, Madonna, Buster Keaton, Chris Bonnington, Brian Deighton (my car mechanic), Billy Elliot, Claire Francis

Ten ways to use or develop your bodily-kinesthetic intelligence

1. Write and act out dramatic sketches or improvisations that illustrate aspects of your studies.
2. Learn about Yoga, Tai Chi and other relaxation/meditation techniques.
3. Learn how to juggle (a great 'whole brain' exercise)!
4. Develop a personal 'limbering-up-for-learning' routine.
5. Turn information into physical gestures, the way that children's rhymes have accompanying actions.
6. Try to give somebody directions without using your hands.
7. Learn about different styles of dance and accompanying routines.
8. Take up a sport that involves dexterity or graceful, controlled movement.
9. Play computer games that require you to have quick reflexes.
10. Practise craftwork, pottery, gardening, needlework or any activity that involves making things and movement.

5. LOGICAL MATHEMATICAL Intelligence

This intelligence is shown in the ability to use numbers and to make logical and reasonable judgements based on a rational process of thinking. Typical logical-mathematical intelligence is shown by the scientist, detective and doctor, the accountant and computer programmer, and the ordinary person who is fascinated with 'whodunnits' and number puzzles, chess and computer games.

Logical-mathematical intelligence stars/characters

(You might like to find out more about these people using the Internet.)

Mr Spock, Stephen Hawking, Jonathan Creek, Susan Greenfield, Albert Einstein, Carol Vorderman, Data, Sherlock Holmes

Ten ways to use or develop your logical-mathematical intelligence

1. Practise calculating or estimating things like size, quantity, distance, weight, etc.
2. Watch or read detective-thrillers and try to work out the conclusion.
3. Learn about recent discoveries and developments in popular science (especially connected with science of the brain and learning).
4. Find out about philosophers such as Aristotle and Plato who invented 'philosophy'.
5. Add up the cost of your lunch as you wait in the school dinner/shop queue.
6. Plan and record your personal finances carefully.
7. Keep a detailed school planner, recording work done and homework to be completed. Be systematic about its upkeep.
8. Always look for reasons or evidence to support what you say or write.
9. Use a highlighter/different coloured pen to 'annotate' books you read.
10. Make lists and summaries of information in 'step-by-step' language.

6. INTERPERSONAL Intelligence

This talent is the ability to deal with people, to understand and sympathise with their motives and feelings and to be able to communicate with them effectively. People who counsel others have these skills in great measure, as do teachers, sales people, managers, air-hostesses, nurses, policemen, TV personalities and politicians. Those with interpersonal intelligence are good at motivating people and dealing with their emotional and personal problems and, as in 'Emotional Intelligence', have a great ability to show 'empathy' for other people and their needs.

Interpersonal intelligence stars

(You might like to find out more about these people using the Internet.)

Mother Teresa, Billy Connolly, Bruce Forsyth, William Shakespeare, Alex Ferguson, Princess Diana, Tom Hanks

Ten ways to use or develop your interpersonal intelligence

1. Aim to speak to one person each day to whom you have never spoken before.
2. Teach a topic you have studied to someone else (great for revision).
3. Help to organise a series of activities for entertaining young children.
4. Practise being a chairperson in discussions and debates.
5. Hold brainstorming homework sessions with your friends.
6. 'Adopt' a younger child in the school, listen to them read, encourage them in their work, talk to them about ideas they find difficult.
7. Direct, write or take part in a play. Perform it as entertainment for your family or friends.
8. Spend time watching (discreetly) how people behave towards each other and try to 'read' situations. What is happening?
9. Offer to help somebody else 'catch up' on work they have missed.
10. Take a turn at becoming class 'rep' if you have a school council or a similar pupil forum.

7. INTRAPERSONAL Intelligence

This intelligence is marked by deep thinking, soul-searching and the understanding of our selves and our emotional inner states. People who demonstrate this intelligence in great depth usually engage in 'thinking' pastimes or spend a lot of time at prayer or in some kind of meditation – e.g. clergymen or other devout religious people, philosophers, judges, diarists etc. Again, they exhibit some of the qualities of Emotional Intelligence through 'self-awareness' and are able to analyse their own moods and feelings in order to explain them and come to terms with them.

Intrapersonal intelligence stars

(You might like to find out more about these people using the Internet.)

The Dalai Lama, Bertrand Russell, Alan Bennett, Rabbi Lionel Blue, Plato, John Donne

Ten ways to use or develop your intrapersonal intelligence

1. Keep a diary for a month (possibly not January!) and record your thoughts and feelings about all you see and experience.
2. Write chapters from your autobiography (possibly to be given as a present to your own children one day!).
3. Try to analyse your dreams (what caused me to dream about that?).
4. Read biographies of people who became famous for their strong personalities and beliefs.
5. Every day, write and review affirmations you have made.
6. Find out about different forms of religious worship.
7. Find out about 'philosophy' and the topics it covers.
8. At the end of each day, review the things about that day that went really well. Look forward to the things you are going to achieve the next day.
9. Build up a file of 'Magic Moments' experiences.
10. Take time for yourself each day – as silly as it might sound, try 'talking to yourself' in your mind. Use 'affirmation' talk the way Tiger Woods does to prepare mentally for a challenge ahead.

8. NATURALIST *Intelligence*

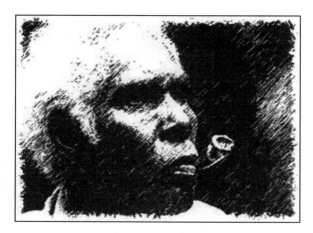

An Aborigine or native of the Amazon rainforest would probably get a PhD in naturalist intelligence. It is the kind of talent shown by people who are close to nature or who have an 'affinity with' nature. This can include sailors, astronomers, farmers, vets, weather forecasters, gardeners, bee-keepers, anthropologists, zoo-keepers etc. They are people who can communicate with and understand animals, understand natural forces and rhythms and find peace and solace in the natural environment.

Naturalist intelligence stars/characters

(You might like to find out more about these people using the Internet.)

Crocodile Dundee, Lee and Gerald Durrell, David Attenborough, Hannah Hawksworth, Tarzan, Alan Titchmarsh, Patrick Moore, Monty Roberts, James Herriot

Ten ways to use or develop your naturalist intelligence

1. Keep a pet and learn about how to keep it healthy and well looked after.
2. Learn about the weather/watch the forecasts and review them each day.
3. Be observant about the kinds of things growing in people's gardens.
4. Watch nature and animal-care programmes and documentaries.
5. Visit zoos and natural history museums.
6. Become an expert in one aspect of nature or animal study (dinosaurs, birds, volcanoes, stars etc.). Give a short talk to your class about the subject of your 'expertise'.
7. Work out a nature trail for young children in an area near to where you live.
8. Collect natural artefacts – cones, shells, leaves etc. – as souvenirs of places you have visited.
9. When on holiday, learn about the marine and wildlife you are likely to see, the weather patterns that might occur, the geography of the country.
10. Help your parents with the gardening!

9. EXISTENTIAL Intelligence

It is through this intelligence, Howard Gardner suggests, that human beings really display what singles them out as a species. When we think about our 'existence', our lives and deaths, the nature and scope of the universe and our place in Space and Time, we are exercising our 'existential' intelligence. When we take part in religious rituals (from any faith) and think about God and matters relating to mortality we are exercising our 'existential' intelligence.

Existential intelligence stars

(You might like to find out more about these people using the Internet.)

The Pope, The Archbishop of Canterbury, The Chief Rabbi, and all other revered religious leaders.

Ten ways to use and develop your existential intelligence

1. Read sacred books that deal with spiritual and existential matters (the Bible, the Koran, Bhagavad Gita, Dhammapada, the writings of Confucius).
2. Learn how to meditate.
3. Watch films that have big moral and existential themes – *Jesus of Nazareth*, *Schindler's List* etc.
4. Read poetry and essays by writers who tackle 'big themes' – Thomas Hardy's poetry, Emily Brontë's *Wuthering Heights*, D. H. Lawrence's 'Phoenix', Walt Whitman's 'Leaves of Grass'.
5. Listen to music written to evoke deep spiritual feelings (Bach, Mozart, Haydn, Vangelis etc.).
6. Keep a record of 'big questions' that occur to you. 'Where was I before I was born?' etc.
7. Read biographies or summaries of great thinkers' lives.
8. Invite leaders from different faiths to talk to your class about their beliefs. Or take turns yourselves.
9. View great works of art that are about life, death, existence and 'soulfulness'.
10. Find out about recent thinking in the science of cosmology and the study of the origin of the universe (the work of Stephen Hawking, Roger Penrose etc.).

Multiple Intelligences: Activities

The Intelligent Channel 'MI evening'

A message from the head of light entertainment

We hope to provide a special evening's schedule of programmes to celebrate twenty years since the publication of *Frames of Mind*, Howard Gardner's celebrated book on Multiple Intelligences. It is your job as producers to make a series of short TV programmes, each of which demonstrates this range of intelligences. This will be broadcast live on_____. Have fun and let's celebrate the diverse range of intelligence in us all!

Suggested items for this special evening of mixed light entertainment

1. *Professor Brent Tug's Annual Open University 'Burnett Lecture'*
   'The Seven Ages of Man' (from the play *As You like It* by William Shakespeare) – a reading of the extract, followed by a short talk on its meaning.

2. *Sister Cindy's Picture Feature*
   A short lecture on the meaning of a chosen work of art, including biographical information about the artist and explanatory and background information on the work chosen.

3. *Poetry? Yes Please!*
   Today's guest chooses a poem and reads it aloud to suitable background music and pictures.

4. *Comedy Store*
   Jokes, laughter and comedy routines from these class acts.

5. *Creature Feature*
   Animal special – 'The care of my pet'.

6. *Ricci Fake*
   Controversial discussion programme with today's theme: 'What should education be like in the 21st century?'

7. *Who Wants to Be a Go-zillionaire?*
    More hopefuls battle for the prize in this year's final. Tonight's contestants include one who is answering questions only on 'the human brain'!

8. *Stars in Your Eyes*
    Karaoke and dance stars perform in this year's final.

9. *News*
    A video-magazine documentary about news (about your school).

10. *Nosey Parkinson*
    Chat-show superstar Norman 'Nosey' Parkinson interviews tonight's celebrity guests.

Review

This show might be performed to another class, recorded on video and played back for you (or possibly your parents) to review. Live is best! No second takes! Please send copies of finished videos to Garry Burnett at Malet Lambert School, Hull. All videos will be viewed, reviewed and thoroughly enjoyed!

Question

Which are the dominant intelligences exercised in each activity?

Activities

1. Use all the information you have learnt about MI to plan a revision programme for a subject you have studied this term. How will you use all of your intelligences and a range of VAK stimulus to make your revision more effective?
2. Your best friend has been away from school and knows nothing about the idea of MI. Prepare some notes and an explanation of the lessons he or she has missed.

Multiple Intelligences: Conclusions

A Balanced Profile

In many of the examples you will find that two or more intelligences were probably being used to 'solve the problem' or 'create or perform something'. None of these talents 'stands alone', and to have a complete and discerning intelligence profile we need to be effective at using all of them at different times and in different strengths.

So let us *affirm* that we will seek to develop balanced intelligence profiles in order to make ourselves very powerful and successful learners of all new information.

Unlike the savant, we will strive not to be good just at one at the expense of all of the others.

We know that truly intelligent people can exercise all of their intelligences whenever they choose to live happy and effective lives.

Representational Languages

Each one of these multiple intelligences has its own special language – which means there is a unique *way* that each intelligence can be expressed. How you choose to represent your intelligence will be evident by the representations that you make (the way you choose to do something).

Extension Activities

MI: Multiple Intelligences or Mission Impossible?

Try to assess which of the range of multiple intelligences you need to use to perform the following tasks successfully. All tasks must be attempted!

MI Task 1

This extract is taken from Gilbert and Sullivan's Opera *The Pirates of Penzance*. Your task is to read and understand the extract, find out what all of the references mean, find a recording of the piece and listen to how it is phrased; *then* to read the lyrics out loud with gestures, without making a mistake. Do you accept your mission?

A Modern Major-General

I am the very model of a modern Major-General,
I've information vegetable, animal, and mineral,
I know the kings of England, and I quote the fights historical
From Marathon to Waterloo, in order categorical;
I'm very well acquainted, too, with matters mathematical,
I understand equations, both the simple and quadratical,
About binomial theorem I'm teeming with a lot o' news,
With many cheerful facts about the square of the hypotenuse.
I'm very good at integral and differential calculus;
I know the scientific names of beings animalculous:
In short, in matters vegetable, animal, and mineral,
I am the very model of a modern Major-General.

I know our mythic history, King Arthur's and Sir Caradoc's;
I answer hard acrostics, I've a pretty taste for paradox,
I quote in elegiacs all the crimes of Heliogabalus,
In conics I can floor peculiarities parabolous;
I can tell undoubted Raphaels from Gerard Dows and Zoffanies,
I know the croaking chorus from the Frogs of Aristophanes!
Then I can hum a fugue of which I've heard the music's din afore,
And whistle all the airs from that infernal nonsense Pinafore.

Then I can write a washing bill in Babylonic cuneiform,
And tell you ev'ry detail of Caractacus's uniform:
In short, in matters vegetable, animal, and mineral,
I am the very model of a modern Major-General.

In fact, when I know what is meant by "mamelon" and "ravelin",
When I can tell at sight a Mauser rifle from a javelin,
When such affairs as sorties and surprises I'm more wary at,
And when I know precisely what is meant by "commissariat",
When I have learnt what progress has been made in modern gunnery,
When I know more of tactics than a novice in a nunnery

In short, when I've a smattering of elemental strategy,
You'll say a better Major-General has never sat a gee.
For my military knowledge, though I'm plucky and adventury,
Has only been brought down to the beginning of the century;
But still, in matters vegetable, animal, and mineral,
I am the very model of a modern Major-General.

(Sir Arthur Sullivan, from *The Pirates of Penzance*)

MI Task 2

Can you solve the following puzzles?

1. A man stands in front of a painting and says to his son: "Brothers and sisters have I none but that man's father is my father's son." How is the man in the painting related to the man standing in front of it?
2. The day before yesterday Freda was seventeen. Next year she will be twenty. How can this be so?
3. A man stood looking through the window of the 63rd floor of an office building. Suddenly he was overcome by an impulse. He opened the window. It was a sheer drop outside the building to the ground. He did not use a parachute or land in water or on any special, soft surface. Yet he was completely unhurt when he landed. How could this be so?

MI Task 3

Prepare and tape-record a 3-minute 'Thought for the day' broadcast for BBC Radio 4. Listen to current broadcasts (around 7.50 am) and note the language and style used and the kind of issues covered.

MI Task 4

Translate the following speech into modern English and then answer the questions on it.

'The Seven Ages of Man'

JAQUES:
All the world's a stage,
And all the men and women merely players:
They have their exits and their entrances;
And one man in his time plays many parts,
His acts being seven ages. At first the infant,
Mewling and puking in the nurse's arms.
And then the whining school-boy, with his satchel
And shining morning face, creeping like snail
Unwillingly to school. And then the lover,
Sighing like furnace, with a woeful ballad
Made to his mistress' eyebrow. Then a soldier,
Full of strange oaths and bearded like the pard,
Jealous in honour, sudden and quick in quarrel,
Seeking the bubble reputation
Even in the cannon's mouth. And then the justice,
In fair round belly with good capon lined,
With eyes severe and beard of formal cut,
Full of wise saws and modern instances;
And so he plays his part. The sixth age shifts
Into the lean and slipper'd pantaloon,
With spectacles on nose and pouch on side,
His youthful hose, well saved, a world too wide
For his shrunk shank; and his big manly voice,
Turning again toward childish treble, pipes
And whistles in his sound. Last scene of all,
That ends this strange eventful history,
Is second childishness and mere oblivion,
Sans teeth, sans eyes, sans taste, sans everything.

(William Shakespeare, from *As You Like It*)

1. What does Jaques say the 'seven ages of man' are?
2. What kind of intelligence does Jaques show through his speech?

'VAK' – Learning in Style

Every single one of us has a preferred way of learning, which is based on the way that we use our senses to perceive and process information in situations at school or indeed anywhere. Effective learners can adapt their style to suit the learning situation. A given learning situation might require any of the following modes of perception:

Visual	How we see things
Auditory	How we hear things
Kinesthetic	How we use our bodies or sense of touch to make or do things

All of our senses are important because they give us vital information about the world around us (including taste and smell) but arguably most 'academic' learning does not rely on the use of these senses to help us process information the way the others do.

You should have completed your learning-style profile, which is a good indicator of the preferred way of learning that you may have developed and of the kinds of thing you can do to develop areas in which you are not so strong. You should stick the print-out of your learning-style profile into your exercise book.

The crucial thing about Learning to Learn and becoming a better learner is being able to 'adapt' your learning style to suit the situation you are trying to learn in.

One good example of this is in the 'SpellCAM' section in Chapter Fourteen. A good speller uses a mostly 'visual' style of learning in order to remember how words look. An unsuccessful speller will use a less effective learning style such as making 'auditory' or 'sound' connections. If, for example, you are trying to learn how to spell the word "psychology" and you write it as it 'sounds', you might well come up with something like "sicollegey". So a more appropriate learning style for this situation is 'visual'.

No learning style is any more important than another. The way we 'get the information' about a topic is entirely up to us but we, as good learners, should know that if one way is not working we should try others. A good affirmation to make might be "I am adaptable to any new learning situation" or "I am good at finding new ways of learning". Here is an exercise to help you think about what some of those ways might be.

Activities

The following list is a selection of 'visual', 'auditory' and 'kinesthetic' activities used in teaching and learning. Sort them into 'VAK' categories and then add at least three more activities of your own.

Use this list to help you get the information you need next time you want to learn something new.

Ideas for using visual, auditory and kinesthetic ways of learning

- Paired discussion
- CD-Roms, websites
- Dramatic readings (aloud)
- Use of visual displays in the classroom or corridor
- Videos, photographs, posters, DVDs
- PowerPoint presentations
- Opportunities for talk
- Coloured pens/paper
- Guest speakers
- Mindmap the topic
- Lighting of the room (particularly the importance of daylight)
- Props, illustrations, diagrams
- Tapes
- Hands-on, experiential learning
- Gestures, signs and symbols, facial expressions
- Interactive white-board presentations
- Overhead-projector presentations
- Group discussion
- Design and make activities
- Drama/role plays
- Use of music
- Use of props, artefacts
- Chanting/singing
- Rhythmical or choral reading/improvisation
- Drama, movement, mime
- Visits or field-trips
- Practical demonstrations
- Movement to 'break up' learning
- Use of technology (video-cameras, recording equipment, gadgets and gizmos)

Putting it into practice

Using the list 'Ideas for using visual, auditory and kinesthetic ways of learning', come up with a good way of teaching a novice any three of the following:

1. The rules for a free kick in football
2. How to iron a shirt
3. The names of the Tudor monarchs
4. The order of the planets from Mercury to Pluto (see video)
5. How to count to ten in a foreign language

Transfer the use of this information to the subjects you are studying in school. How can you make learning more effective by increasing the number of ways that you present the information? You might also try to visit the excellent CHAMPS website developed by Colin Rose, www.learntolearn.org.

Chapter Fourteen
Learning to Learn

Memory

In this section you will learn how to use three important memory strategies, which will enhance your memory and accelerate your ability to learn and remember.

The three strategies are:

Chunking	Breaking things down into sections, groups or categories in order to recall them more easily
Association	Using the brain's natural instinct to connect and link information, including the use of a 'peg' system
Mnemonics	Using fun rhymes and acrostics, stories, jingles and songs to hook information to

Notice that this spells the word 'CAM'.

In the next section you will apply this technique to 'spelling'.

Broadly speaking, there are thought to be three kinds of memory that we use in the course of our lives. These are:

Episodic	Episodes in time, conversations, incidents
Procedural	How to do something, make something, play something etc.
Semantic	Names of things, dates, words, trivia, facts etc.

You might be able to think of more categories, and probably more examples to go in them, but in this book these are the three groups that we will be working with. What different memory techniques might we need for each of the three memory categories?

Activities

'He who has learned to learn ...'

Watch the 'Introduction to memory' on the 'Learning to Learn' video. Then read this account of the way the actor Anthony 'Hannibal' Hopkins remembers lines and answer the questions that follow:

In his book *Wise-Up*, Guy Claxton writes about the amazing ability to memorise lines possessed by that huge star of stage and screen Sir Anthony Hopkins. Apparently, while filming Steven Spielberg's *Amistad* he was able to remember 7 pages of lines without a break and to get them right first time when he was filmed. But this is not an ability that he was born with, Sir Anthony has learned how to use his memory effectively. He has learned to learn. This is how Guy Claxton says he does it:

> "He reads each line over three hundred times, annotating the script with the number of times he has read the section so far. As his recall improves he makes a cross in the margin, then a star out of the cross, and then puts a ring around the star. The script is covered with hand-drawn images, executed in multi-coloured felt-tip; landscapes, faces, incidents ranging from the Gothic to the futuristic. The lines themselves are highlighted in green, yellow and blue – orange and red for violent scenes. Hopkins' memory is not an innate talent ; it reflects a mastery of learning."

(Guy Claxton, from *Wise Up*)

1. Why do you think Anthony Hopkins's methods are successful?
2. Discuss with your partner any strategies for remembering that you have.
3. Describe techniques you have for remembering pin numbers, telephone numbers, combination-lock numbers, shopping lists, people's names etc.

Test your short-term memory – 'Swap Shop'

Sit in a circle in your classroom. Everyone should think of a book they have read recently. When the teacher gives the signal you should all stand up and pretend you are swapping books. Tell the other person the name of your book and listen and take their book-title from them. Then repeat the process, this time passing on the title you have just been given, with as many people as you can in *one minute*.

Sit back round in the circle and in turn call out the name of the book you started with. See who has your book now.

There is a strong possibility that only a handful of the 'most memorable' titles will still be in circulation. The rest will have disappeared!

Try repeating the exercise with people's names, record titles, etc. Work out strategies for achieving 100% success in this difficult game.

The name game

Work in groups of 5–7. Sit in a circle facing each other. Each person thinks of a positive alliterative adjective to describe themselves. For example, 'Marvellous Malcolm', 'Nice Narinder', and so on. (The stranger the better.)

Take turns in going round the group and trying to call out each person's name. When everybody can say all of the rest of their group's names and their adjectives they should do so in front of the whole class.

If done properly, each group will represent a 'chunk' of the whole class. Their 'adjectives' are a kind of association technique that should add emotional content to the memory.

See who can recall the whole class's names and their accompanying adjectives.

Test your memory!

How good do you think your memory is? Test yourself!

First, say whether the statements below are true or not true. Be as honest as you can:

I find it difficult to remember the correct equipment for school.	True/not true
I find it difficult to remember routes and maps.	True/not true
I find it hard to remember the names of my favourite pop stars.	True/not true
I find it hard to remember the names of famous people from history.	True/not true
I find it hard to remember how many days there are in each month.	True/not true
I find spelling some words difficult.	True/not true
I do not think it is possible to improve your memory.	True/not true
We remember every single event in our lives.	True/not true
I can improve my memory and have some fun as well.	True/not true
If my memory were good it would help me to be a better learner.	True/not true

Discuss these results with your partner. You might share the answers you gave with the whole class.

Most people would agree that having a good memory is important for learning, but many of us do not believe that it is possible to do much about improving our memories. This is certainly not the case, as you will see. There are ways to improve your memory – and to have fun while doing so.

Some Frequently Asked Questions About Memory

Is it possible to improve our memories?

Definitely YES! As you will find in this book, there is nothing to stop each of us developing our memory and becoming a great 'memoriser'.

Do we really remember every single event that has ever happened in our lives?

The latest scientific evidence points to the answer that we do. We store away every single sight, sound, smell and experience that has happened to us since we were born and many from before we were born! The problem is *recall*.

Are our memories really more powerful than those of a computer?

Yes, they are, and what is more our memories are quicker than a computer – if we know how to use them.

Can improving my memory be easy and fun?

It can be if you know how to do it. Improving your memory need not be boring or hard work. It can be fun and can help you feel much more confident about yourself.

If my memory were better would it help me learn more?

Almost certainly YES! Most of the new subjects you will learn at secondary school will require that you use your memory. You might be asked to remember a list of events in History, some new words in Languages or a formula in Science. The better your memory, the easier it will be to learn in these subjects.

Does having a good memory mean you are more intelligent?

Not on its own. Having a good memory is just one of the thinking skills an intelligent person will use. As we saw with the 'savant', not being able to do anything with the information other than 'echo' what you have seen or heard is not enough to help you solve problems and meet challenges in life.

Being 'flexible' with information is a more effective way of demonstrating your intelligence, and that means being able to *transfer* what you have learnt to other situations.

How can I start to improve my memory?

To begin with it will be useful to find out how your memory is working at the moment. Here is an exercise to help you understand that process.

Study the items on the following page. There are twenty of them. Give yourself two minutes to do so. After two minutes, try to write down as many as you can without looking. No cheating!

Memory Skills

Memory Skills Answer Sheet

Now try to list as many of the twenty items as you can.

1. _____
2. _____
3. _____
4. _____
5. _____
6. _____
7. _____
8. _____
9. _____
10. _____
11. _____
12. _____
13. _____
14. _____
15. _____
16. _____
17. _____
18. _____
19. _____
20. _____

Now turn back and tick the ones that you remembered correctly. Add up how many you got right and see what your score says about your memory.

15–20 You already have a very good memory and should be looking for ways to make your memory excellent.

10–15 Your memory is about average, but not nearly as good as it could be.

0–10   You will find the work we are going to do in this booklet really useful and your memory will be much improved by the end of the unit.

Test yourself again on the twenty items following the work you are now about to do in order to see what a difference it can make.

Reflection

One of the ways that we become better learners is to reflect on (look back on) the way we learned something to see how successful it was.

- Did we use an appropriate learning style?
- Were we using our intelligences?
- *How* did we try to remember these things this time?
- What methods did we use?
- Which of the objects was the easiest to remember? Why?

Our short-term memory can only possibly handle seven items at once unless we do something special with the information. Just staring at the items will not make a difference to how well we remember them; we need to use our knowledge of how the brain and our intelligences work to make the change.

Now we will begin the 'something special' that will help all of you remember all twenty of the objects – if you choose to do so.

Chunking

One of the easiest methods of improving your memory is to group things together into 'sets' or 'chunks'.

Chunking is a way of working with the brain's natural instinct to search for patterns and order. That is why things are easier to remember when they are filed in this way.

Look carefully at the following numbers:

52365123130282460602002

If we had to remember those numbers for any reason our instinct would be automatically to search for some kind of pattern before we record the information in our long-term memories.

Look again at the same numbers:

52 365 12 31 30 28 24 60 60 2002

Can you begin to see a pattern now? *The clue is 'time' and a 'year'.*

If you think back to the twenty items on the sheet, did you guess that the items might be able to be put in groups of five? Think carefully about what the titles of those groups might be and complete the following chart. When you have chunked the items on the memory test sheet, try the test again to see if your score improves.

For use with Memory Exercise

Category	Objects				

Association

As you have seen from our work on the brain, the association cortex is constantly looking for opportunities to connect information and link it to other networks of meaning. Association means to 'link' together.

Sometimes we can 'hook' an important piece of information through a visual, auditory or kinesthetic learning technique and record it very powerfully. Take this example of counting to ten in German.

First the 'traditional' way:

Number	German
1	eins
2	zwei
3	drei
4	vier
5	fünf
6	sechs
7	sieben
8	acht
9	neun
10	zehn

Now add some *auditory* information:

1. eins (pronounced)	ines
2. zwei	svigh
3. drei	dry
4. vier	fear
5. fünf	foonf
6. sechs	sex
7. sieben	see ben
8. acht	act
9. neun	noyn
10. zehn	sane

Now add some *kinesthetic* information:

		gesture
1. eins	ines	point to eyes
2. zwei	svigh	spy with binoculars
3. drei	dry	rub your arm dry
4. vier	fear	be frightened
5. fünf	foonf	punch
6. sechs	sex	wolf-whistle
7. sieben	see ben	look for a boy called Ben
8. acht	act	dramatic gesture
9. neun	noyn	boing, on springs
10. zehn	sane	make a speech bubble, 'saying'

Practise this until you can recite the numbers confidently.

Associating the action with the word will make very powerful connections and enable you to recall the information in a different way.

Activity

Now try learning other information in the same way: Try counting in French, Spanish or whichever language you are studying. Learn a string of historical information; or perhaps some information from Science.

Peg-systems

These are another form of 'association', which work when you connect the information you wish to learn with another object and gesture.

The pegs in this system are taken from the children's rhyme 'This Old Man'.

This old man, he played ... he played knick knack on my ...

Peg	Action	Connection – information to learn
1 Tum	Touch your stomach	
2 Shoe	Tap your shoe	
3 Knee	Rub your knee	
4 Door	Knock on the door	
5 Hive	Wave away the bees	
6 Sticks	Play drum sticks	
7 Heaven	Say a prayer	
8 Gate	Open the gate	
9 Line	Hang out the washing	
10 Hen	Feed the chickens	

Practise the gestures until you can confidently go through the full system without making a mistake.

So how do we use pegs to learn?

The important thing is to let the pegs *suggest* the information to you. For example, if you needed to learn the safety rules for a Science laboratory, you might use the pegs in the following way:

Learning Science lab safety rules using a peg-system

1. Tie back long hair and fasten loose clothing
   (wrap your really long hair around your tummy three times)

2. Always wear safety equipment such as goggles
   (look at your tapping foot through your very large goggles)

3. Never run in the laboratory
   (rub your knee, which you hurt as you fell in the laboratory, running!)

4. Do not leave bags and coats on the floor
   (imagine not being able to get into the classroom because the bags and coats are piled up against the door)

5. Know what to do in case of fire
   (as you waved away the bees before, wave away the smoke from the fire)

And, of course, you can have great fun making the association more and more bizarre, emotional, and therefore 'memorable'.

Practise using the peg-system on the following information:

- The equipment you need to bring to lessons
- Your timetable!
- Any other information, from any subject, that will need 'pegging' in your long-term memory

Mnemonics, Jingles and Rhymes

Activities

1. What does each of the following mnemonics, jingles or rhymes teach us?
    a) Never Eat Shredded Wheat
    b) In 1492 Columbus sailed the ocean blue
    c) Every Good Boy Deserves Favour
    d) Richard of York Gave Battle in Vain
    e) Thirty Days has September,
        April, June and November.
        All the rest have thirty-one
        Except February, alone.

    This kind of language 'play' can be a very powerful way of remembering. It uses linguistic and musical intelligence to reinforce the learning.

    'Never Eat Cake Eat Salad Sandwiches And Remain Young' is a very useful way of remembering how many 'c's and 's's there are in the word 'necessary'.

2. Write down any other mnemonics, jingles or rhymes that you have found helpful.

3. Try to make up similar mnemonics for things that you may need to remember (facts or formulas in Maths or Science; facts or events in History; or other key pieces of information).

SpellCAM

We will now apply some of the memory techniques you have learnt to 'spelling'.

Background Theory – Summary

There are lots of complicated new words you will be expected to learn in Key Stage Three – too many to write down here. So what you really need is a 'way' of learning new spellings that you can use with any word you come across, in any subject. The work you did in the section on 'Memory' will now be put to the test in this section.

Remember the three very powerful ways of working with your brain and using your intelligences to learn that we studied. These were:

Chunking	This involves breaking things down into smaller components and looking for patterns.
Association	This means connecting the new information to something you have already learnt.
Mnemonics	These can use humour or emotion to hook the new learning to long-term memory.

How to Learn to Spell

Try using the following approach to learning spellings in the future.

Step 1: appraise the situation

Ask "Which part of the word do I need to learn?". If you misspell a word, look carefully at the parts of the word spelt correctly, and the parts of the word you misspelt *this time*. Affirm that you will always spell the word correctly in the future and tell yourself that the mistake was a mere temporary 'setback'. Congratulate yourself for the letters you did get in the correct place and order.

Step 2: action

Then review the word in any of the following ways:

A. Chunking

Take a word like *Caterpillar*. How many words can you see inside the word (cat, pill, pillar, ill, at, ate, cater)? Make them into a saying: "My *cat ate* a *pill* and *was ill* behind a *pillar*. I cannot *cater* for her!"

Or take the word *friend*: "A *friend* will always be there in the end."
Remember *separate* has *a rat* in it!
Imagine *abundance* (plenty) as *a bun dance*!

Activity

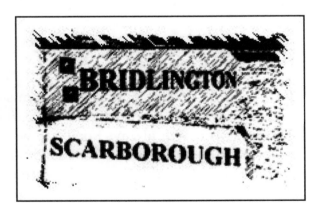

Make a list of 20 words that have other words inside them. Write the other words in a different colour. Here are three words to help you start. (You should write the 'other' words in a different colour.)

Safeway	(Safe, few, way)
Manchester	(Man, chest)
Scarborough	(Scar, car, rough)

Then make up a 'silly sentence' with each of the 'found words' in, for example: "There are *few ways* I cannot feel *safe* in Safeway!"

B. Association

Learning to count in German meant associating the word with a physical action in order for it to be encoded on to our long-term memory systems. As you know, this kind of 'connecting' to something else is very effective because it works with the brain's natural way of linking information to other knowledge.

Take the word 'shoe' – which does not look at all like how it sounds ('shoo'). If I wanted to learn to spell 'shoe', one way I could learn it by association would be to connect it to words I can already spell that have an identical letter string. For example:

Shoe
Toe
Foe
Hoe
Does

Silly sentence: "I nearly lost my *toe* when a *foe* took a **hoe** and chopped my *shoe* – what *does* he think he's doing?"

Remember, you may *"hear with your <u>ear</u>"*.

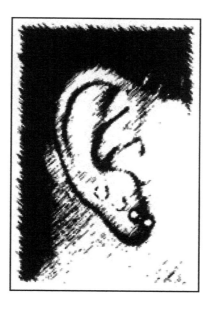

You could link a word like 'la<u>ugh</u>ter' with 'f<u>igh</u>t', 't<u>igh</u>t', 'm<u>igh</u>t' and 's<u>igh</u>t'.

Activity
Find words you can associate with each of the following:

Here	**dis**appear	**sch**ool	sens**ible**
There	dis	sch	ible
Where	dis	sch	ible

C. Mnemonic, Jingles and Rhymes

Using emotion (humour, surprise etc.) can help create powerful memories (note the section on memory on the video).

Take a word like 'beautiful' – which has what could be a tricky beginning: 'beau'. If you were to make a mnemonic such as:

Bad
Eggs
Are
Useless

it might help you to remember the order of that letter 'string'.

"One chips and two sausages" can be very helpful when trying to spell 'necessary', because there is one 'c' and two 's's!

Activities

- Write down any other 'fun' mnemonics, jingles or rhymes that you know for remembering spellings.
- Design an A4 poster that will help teach someone how to spell a new word. A cartoon illustration will help bring the idea to life.

Step 3: show you know

- *Cover* the word from view and try to see it on the inside of your eyelids.
- *Say* the word aloud.
- *Write* the word down.
- *Check* it, and
- *Repeat* the process – the more repetitions the better (remember Anthony Hopkins's way of learning lines)!

Activity

Practise the following short dictation on each other. Then devise ways of learning the words in it so that you can spell them all correctly. Remember, it is not so much the new spellings as the techniques that we are interested in. Once you have learnt to learn to spell you can apply these techniques to any new learning situation.

"I bought a turquoise ukulele from a character outside the stationery shop adjacent to the Coliseum. I frequently give recitals of medieval compositions in Vienna." (25 words)

Multiply your score by four to give you a percentage.

Test yourself or ask your parents, relatives or friends to test you and see how quickly you can improve your score.

Chapter Fifteen
Evaluation and Review

1. Now that you have finished this 'Learning to Learn' book, think back to the lessons you have had over the course.
2. Which of the topics that you have covered this year has been of the most use to you?
3. Which have you found less useful?
4. Have you used any of the techniques and information you have learnt in any other subjects?
5. Describe briefly how the techniques have helped you to become better at learning in these subjects.
6. Write a letter to a pupil in a lower year describing what 'Learning to Learn' means and how it can help you to be a better learner.

Conclusion

After completing this introductory module in 'Learning to Learn' you should have a very different outlook on how you learn, and on how you prepare the right state of mind in order to approach positively and confidently any new learning situation.

You should be able to:

1. Use techniques such as 'making affirmations' to set very positive and ambitious targets for yourself
2. Know how to create a positive and confident state of mind in order to face new challenges
3. Have a very positive view of the future and your ability to make changes for yourself
4. Benchmark people who have already been successful in areas where you want to grow and change
5. Feel more confident about taking risks in order to make changes and step out of your comfort zone
6. Understand more about the style of learning you prefer to operate in
7. Understand the different kinds of intelligence and know how to use and develop these effectively
8. Understand that through emotional intelligence we can not only be more positive and effective as learners but also we can understand the needs of others
9. Find out ways of making any learning interesting and relevant to you
10. Have great fun learning!

In Module 2 we will explore further ways of helping you think more effectively about how to learn best.

Glossary

Affirmation	A way of writing or thinking that makes a strong personal vow to do something.
Auditory	Connected with sounds.
Axon	The arm that shoots out from the neuron and looks to make connections with other neurons.
Benchmarking	Looking up to someone as an example or 'model'.
Comfort zone	A routine, place or habit you feel comfortable with.
Dendrite	The tiny connecting bud that grows from the axon.
Kinesthetic	Connected with touch and the body.
Learning style	Your preferred way of doing something in order to learn.
Limbic	The area of the brain where emotions and long-term memories are formed.
Multiple Intelligences	Theories, made popular by Howard Gardner, that state the belief that human beings have many different ways of demonstrating that they are clever.
Neurons	Brain cells.
Psychology	The study of the mind.
Reptilian	In evolution, the oldest area of the brain responsible for many of our automatic and instinctive responses.
Reticular Formation	The area of the brain that filters important information and directs things to our attention.
Synapse	The electro-chemical firing between neurons that takes place when connections have been made and new information has been learnt.
Triune	A theory, made popular by the scientist Paul McLean, that states the belief that the brain operates on three different levels; reptilian, limbic and neo-cortex.
Neo-cortex	A part of the brain that is sometimes known as the 'thinking cap'.
VAK	visual, auditory and kinesthetic.
Visual	Connected with sight, vision.

Bibliography

Angelou, Maya (1995). *The Collected Poems of Maya Angelou*, London, Virago Press.

Armstrong, Thomas (2000). *7 Kinds of Smart: Identifying and Developing Your Multiple Intelligences*, London, Plume Books.

Brearley, Michael (2001). *Emotional Intelligence in the Classroom*, Carmarthen, Crown House Publishing.

Burnett, Garry (1995). *Twenty Six Baboons and Other Stories*, Hull, Magpie Publishing.

Buzan, Tony (2001). *The Mind Map Book: Millennium Edition*, London, BBC Consumer Publishing.

Buzan, Tony (2000). *Head First: Ten Ways to Tap into Your Natural Genius*, London, Harper Collins.

Claxton, Guy (2001). *Wise Up: The Challenge of Lifelong Learning*, Stafford, Network Educational Press.

Claxton, Guy (2000). *Hare Brain, Tortoise Mind: Why Intelligence Increases When You Think Less*, New York, Ecco Press.

Curtis Richard et al (1999). *Blackadder: The Whole Damn Dynasty: 1485–1917*, London, Penguin Books.

Dryden, Gordon and Jeanette Vos (2001). *Learning Revolution*, Stafford, Network Educational Press.

Gardner, Howard ([1983 Basic Books] 1993). *Frames of Mind: The Theory of Multiple Intelligences*, London, Fontana.

Gardner, Howard (1993). *Multiple Intelligences: The Theory in Practice*, Oxford, Basic Books.

Gardner, Howard (2000). *Intelligence Reframed: Multiple Intelligence For the 21st Century*, Oxford, Basic Books.

Gardner, Howard (2000). *The Disciplined Mind: Beyond Facts and Standardized Tests*, New Jersey, Penguin Books.

Ginnis, Paul (2002). *The Teacher's Toolkit: Raise Classroom Achievement with Activities For Every Learner*, Carmarthen, Crown House Publishing.

Goleman, Daniel (1996). *Emotional Intelligence: Why it Matters More Than IO*, London, Bloomsbury.

Greenfield, Susan (1994). *The Royal Institution Christmas Lectures: Journey to the Centre of the Brain*, London, BBC.

Jensen, Eric (1995). *Brain-Based Learning*, San Diego, California, The Brain Store Inc.

Jensen, Eric (1997). *Neuro-Tour: A Guide To The Human Brain*, San Diego, California, The Brain Store Inc.

Jensen, Eric (1998). *Teaching with the Brain In Mind*, Tunbridge Wells, Kent, Atlantic Books.

Layton, George (2000). *A Northern Childhood*, London, Longman.

Lazear, David (1994). *Seven Pathways of Learning: Teaching with Students and Parents about Multiple Intelligences*, Tuscon, Arizona, Zephyr Press.

Lucas, Bill (2001). *Power Up Your Mind: Learn Faster, Work Faster*, London, Nicholas Brealey Publishing.

Lucas, George (1999). *Star Wars: The Empire Strikes Back: The Complete, Fully Illustrated Script*, London, Virgin Books.

Owen, Gareth (1985). *Song of the City*, London, Collins.

Rose, Colin (1992). *Accelerate Your Learning*, Aylesbury, Bucks, Accelerated Learning Systems.

Rose, Colin and Malcolm J. Nicholl (1997). *Accelerated Learning For The 21st Century*, New York, Dell Publishing.

Rose, Colin (1999). *Master if Faster*, Aylesbury, Bucks, Accelerated Learning Systems.

Smith, Alistair (1996). *Accelerated Learning in the Classroom*, Stafford, Network Educational Press.

Strege, John (1998). *Tiger: A Biography of Tiger Woods*, New York, Broadway Books.

Tice, Lou (1989). *Investment in Excellence*, Seattle, The Pacific Institute.

Tice, Lou (1991). *Strategic Thinking for Strategic Planning*, Seattle, The Pacific Institute.

Treffert, Darrold A. (1989). *Extraordinary People*, London, Black Swan Publishing.

Young, Cliff (1995). *Cliffy's Book*, Stratford, Australia, High Country Publishing.

Michael Brearley

Emotional Intelligence in the Classroom

CREATIVE LEARNING STRATEGIES FOR 11–18 YEAR OLDS

photocopiable resource

ISBN: 978-189983665-9

This teaching resource aptly demonstrates how pupils can approach their work, and their future, with confidence, ambition, optimism and integrity. Providing practical strategies for integrating Emotional Intelligence across the curriculum, Emotional Intelligence in the Classroom reveals the power of emotion in learning. It explains the fundamentals of Emotional Intelligence (EI) and Emotional Quotient (EQ) and presents original research on the impact of EI on learning

A thoroughly practical work, containing numerous reproducible resources for the classroom teacher.

"Michael Brearley has provided a succinct and readable summary of what Emotional Intelligence can offer to the learning repertoire of children. In a clear and accessible style the book draws on the theory of emotional and multiple intelligence and pins this down into a series of structured activities for classrooms. This book is a must for those who are serious about a multi-layered approach to learning."

Alistair Smith, Author and leading educational trainer

"*Emotional Intelligence in the Classroom* by Michael Brearley provides a clear account of some practical strategies for integrating emotional intelligence across the school curriculum."

Professor Katherine Ware, Health Education

Former headmaster Michael Brearley is widely experienced in secondary education, and has a long-standing interest in engaging students more fully in their learning. Brearley's applied research at the University of East Anglia (UK) focused on teacher behaviour and how it impacted on students' learning; a later study examined the role of mediation and the work of Carl Rogers. His recent research into Emotional Intelligence has explored its practical application in the business and educational sectors, particularly its effect upon performance as a teacher and leader.

www.crownhouse.co.uk

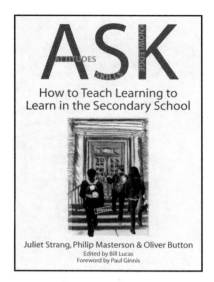

ISBN: 978-184590024-3

Villiers High is one of the first secondary schools in the country to introduce a fully developed curriculum designed so that students can learn how to learn. The results have been remarkable, with year on year improvements in public examination results and an increased student hunger to learn.

ASK: How to Teach Learning-to-Learn in the Secondary School is a serious exploration of the new science of learning. Full of tried and tested teaching and learning strategies, this book will transform the way any teacher sees their subject. All of the lesson ideas detailed in this book are easily applied to any curriculum subject and if used across different subjects, quickly become a transferable map which can help students make sense of their learning and progress rapidly at secondary school.

"…a treasure-trove of material… I heartily commend [this] book to you. It is the real work of real teachers in a real school. They have forged an approach to the nation's most pressing education issue that translates the theory and rhetoric into classroom action. You can adopt their template or customise it; you can read this book as a stimulating case study or as a blueprint. Either way, it will enrich your thinking and practice and ultimately bring great benefits to your students."

Paul Ginnis, trainer and best selling author of *The Teacher's Toolkit*

Juliet Strang is headteacher of Villiers High School an 11-16 comprehensive school in Southall, West London. She has taught in five schools in different parts of the country, including as Assistant Headteacher at George Abbot School in Surrey and Deputy Headteacher at Cranford Community School in Hounslow before moving to Villiers High School in January 1997.

Philip Masterson is currently working as a Deputy Headteacher at Villiers high School. He is a consultant for the Specialist School's Trust, the Institute of Education and Alite, specialising in Learning to Learn and Personalised Learning.

Oliver Button is Assistant Headteacher at Villiers High School in London. His department recently achieved Lead Department status under the Excellence in Cities initiative.

www.crownhouse.co.uk

ISBN: 978-184590070-0

The Learner's Toolkit is an essential resource for supporting the SEAL framework in secondary schools and for all those teaching 11-16 year olds. It contains everything you need to create truly independent learners, confident and resilient in their ability to learn and learn well. The book contains 52 lessons to teach 52 competencies. Each has teacher's notes on leading the lesson and a CD-ROM in the back of the book has all the student forms and worksheets necessary for the lessons. Lessons include:

- getting to know yourself
- persistence and resilience
- controlling moods
- building brain power
- developing willpower
- prioritising and planning

- taking responsibility for your own life
- setting goals for life
- caring for your mind and body
- asking questions
- pushing yourself out of your comfort zone

Possessing these vital competencies will help students learn better and be able to contribute more effectively in school. It will also enable them to thrive in the increasingly fast-paced world of the 21st Century.

"This book supports the new Secondary Curriculum in its efforts to promote Personal Development and links diversity to the Social Emotional Aspects of Learning (SEAL) Framework for secondary schools. It gives teachers starting points, plans and examples to help them use their own ideas to support the progress of young people in the most vital of all areas of learning ... how to cope with and contribute to the world in which they find themselves.î"

Mick Waters, Director of Curriculum, QCA

Jackie Beere is a consultant trainer and School Improvement partner, having been headteacher at Campion School, Northants. She spent three years as an Advanced Skills Teacher leading and implementing innovative Teaching and Learning initiatives including KS3 and 4 Learning to Learn and Thinking Skills programmes. In November 2002 Jackie was awarded the OBE for her services to education.

www.crownhouse.co.uk

the Magic of Metaphor

Foreword by *Judith DeLozier*

77 Stories for Teachers, Trainers & Thinkers

Nick Owen

ISBN: 978-189983670-3

Already on its third reprint this volume presents a collection of powerful stories designed to engage, inspire and transform the listener as well as the reader. Promoting positive feelings, confidence, direction, vision, they supply a wealth of advice and information on the art of creating metaphor and storytelling.

"This book gives the communicator a refreshing and creative way of cutting through the language barrier of Information Technology and delivering clear messages to often diverse audiences."

Alison Hood, Managing Consultant and Operations Director for the Wholesale Investment Banking Practice

More Magic of Metaphor

Stories for Leaders, Influencers and Motivators

Nick Owen

ISBN: 978-190442441-3

This follow up to Nick's best-selling The Magic of Metaphor explores the power of story to inspire, inform, and transform people's lives. With a particular emphasis on leadership in the very broadest sense of the word, the stories in this collection offer inspiration, inner knowledge, and wisdom. Stories and metaphors are incredibly powerful vehicles through which real change and compassion can be generated in the world, and can be used to influence, motivate, and lead others with elegance and integrity.

www.crownhouse.co.uk

ISBN: 978-189983676-5

The Teacher's Toolkit is designed as a teacher's resource to improve the quality of classroom learning. It is packed with practical classroom strategies and enjoyable learning exercises that will enable you to:

- meet the needs of different learning styles
- add a bit of spice to your teaching;
- stimulate your own creative thinking;
- challenge the most gifted ... and the disruptive
- work out what to do with 9F tomorrow!

Whatever your subject, it will give you workable ways of:

- developing thinking skills;
- delivering the attitudes of citizenship;
- embedding study skills;
- creating true independence.

... all in an inclusive classroom. Drawing on insights from neuroscience, psychology and sociology *The Teacher's Toolkit* also provides:

- an overview of recent thinking about learning;
- 50 varied learning techniques for various subjects and ages;
- practical ideas for managing group work, tackling behaviour and promoting personal responsibility;
- six essential ways of operating in the classroom;
- tools for checking that your practice is in line with the best thinking, from lesson planning to performance management.

A book that you will turn to again and again for ideas, *The Teacher's Toolkit* will broaden the range of your teaching practice and equip you with essential new classroom strategies. Providing the tools you need to create an effective learning environment, *The Teacher's Toolkit* is an invaluable sourcebook, guaranteed to contain that lesson-solution.

www.crownhouse.co.uk

ISBN: 978-190442442-0

Through the various activities in this fully photocopiable book, teachers will have the opportunity to develop their students' multiple intelligences in relation to the use and understanding of English literature. In addition, the activities will develop students' analytical thinking skills and creativity and improve exam performance.

The activities are based on the accompanying audio CD of original stories. These stories provide an exciting but accessible opportunity to develop students' emotional and intellectual responses to fiction and their ability to select and organise information, and read, write and think imaginatively. Particular attention has been paid to ensure that the stories appeal to boys as well as girls. All the activities are described with clear learning objectives for the teacher and student.

"Garry Burnett really knows how to engage and inspire students, and his latest book/CD is a triumph. I only wish he had been my English Teacher!"

Colin Rose

Garry Burnett has spent twenty years working in Yorkshire schools as head of English, LEA advisor and project leader for the Campaign for Learning's project Learning to Learn – Research and Development. He is currently an Advanced Skills Teacher at the Malet Lambert School in Hull. He is actively involved in the national Campaign for Learning and regularly leads training sessions at local, national and international level.